"With humor and honesty, this book cuts to the heart of real issues our teens face! Short chapters with clearly written prayers to pray will leave you encouraged instead of overwhelmed. You'll laugh, you'll identify, and you'll come away having spent a sweet prayer time over a real issue with your teen. Every parent of a teen should have a copy!"

—SUSAN ALEXANDER YATES, author of *And Then I Had Teenagers: Encouragement for Parents of Teens and Preteens*

"*Prayer Changes Teens* goes beyond the fluff to give solid, kingdom principles to be praying into the lives of your teens. Both Janet McHenry's heart for prayer and her love for teens come out loud and clear in this powerful book. I heartily recommend *Prayer Changes Teens* to parents who want to see God shape their teenagers into what he has purposed for them."

—JONATHAN GRAF, editor of *Pray!* magazine

"A treasure! Wisdom presented with heart-naked honesty and framed in a quirky sense of humor. Challenging and, at the same time, comforting. Janet offers a gift to the body of Christ. A book no parent should be without."

—JENNIFER KENNEDY DEAN, founder of the Praying Life Foundation and author of numerous books, including *Legacy of Prayer* and *The Life-Changing Power in the Blood of Christ*

"Janet Holm McHenry powerfully and lovingly coaches us in how to specifically pray for our teenagers. *Prayer Changes Teens* combines humor, personal anecdotes, wise counsel, and practical tips so that we might better understand the struggles and temptations of today's teen. Start praying and see God work. Prayer not only changes our teen; prayer changes us."

—LESLIE VERNICK, director of Christ-Centered Counseling
and author of *How to Act Right When Your Spouse Acts Wrong*

"*Prayer Changes Teens* is a candid, comical look at serious issues facing today's parents. It offers sound, nonjudgmental guidance, private prayers, and thought-provoking questions to stimulate parent-teen discussion. Whether you use it for individual or group study, my advice: Read this book with a yellow highlighter."

—BRENDA NIXON, speaker and author of
Parenting Power in the Early Years

"When our children are young, we talk to them about God. When they are grown, we talk to God about them. Janet provides guidance during those tender teen years when we need to be doing a lot of both. By tickling our funny bones and tugging on our hearts, Janet gives practical and powerful principles on prayer for parents of those mysteriously wonderful metamorphosing creatures known as teenagers!"

—SHARON JAYNES, vice president of Proverbs 31 Ministries,
conference speaker, and author of *Being a Great Mom,*
Raising Great Kids

"Got a teenager who wonders where God is during difficult times? Know a teenager who could use some positive changes in his or her life? Then Janet Holm McHenry's latest book, *Prayer Changes Teens,* is one book you won't want to miss!"

—MARTHA BOLTON, "The Cafeteria Lady" of *Brio* magazine
and author of fifty-three books

PRAYER
CHANGES
TEENS

PRAYER
CHANGES
TEENS

HOW TO PARENT FROM YOUR KNEES

Janet Holm McHenry

WATERBROOK
PRESS

PRAYER CHANGES TEENS
PUBLISHED BY WATERBROOK PRESS
2375 Telstar Drive, Suite 160
Colorado Springs, Colorado 80920
A division of Random House, Inc.

ISBN 1-57856-627-4

Copyright © 2003 by Janet Holm McHenry

Published in association with the literary agency of Janet Kobobel Grant, Books & Such, 4788 Carissa Ave., Santa Rosa, CA 95405.

Library of Congress Cataloging-in-Publication Data
McHenry, Janet Holm.
    Prayer changes teens : how to parent from your knees / Janet Holm McHenry.—1st ed.
        p. cm.
Includes bibliographical references.
    ISBN 1-57856-627-4
    1. Parenting—Religious aspects—Christianity. 2. Parent and teenager—Religious aspects—
Christianity. 3. Parents—Prayer-books and devotions—English. 4. Parent and teenager—Prayer-
books and devotions—English. I. Title.
    BV4529.M3845 2003
    248.8'45—dc21
                                                    2003003585

Printed in the United States of America
2003—First Edition

10 9 8 7 6 5 4 3 2 1

For all the parents who've told me
in a parent-teacher conference,
"I just don't know what to do anymore."
Please know that I'm praying for you.

———————

For my four wonderful kids,
Rebekah, Justin, Joshua, and Bethany,
the joys of my life.
You're going to need this book someday!

———————

For their father, my dear husband, Craig.
I love you very much.

Contents

Words of Thanks

Many thanks and much love go to my husband, Craig, and still-home kids, Joshua and Bethany, who promised they really did like fish sticks and frozen fries every weekend I worked on this book.

I owe lots of hugs and maybe even a small loan to my two older children, Rebekah and Justin, who've allowed me to reveal all the secrets of their teenage years. I warned them, though: "You keep forgetting I'm a writer! Stop giving me those great anecdotes!"

I am privileged to work with some amazingly gifted folks at Water-Brook Press who've allowed me to write the book that's been on my heart for many years. Thank you, Don Pape, Steve Cobb, Laura Barker, and the terrific sales and publicity teams.

I couldn't write without the prayer support of my prayer team, my One Heart writer friends, and my friends from the Advanced Writers and Speakers Association (www.awsawomen.com). Thank you for holding me up.

Finally, I am so grateful for my agent friend, Janet Kobobel Grant, who wouldn't let this book dream die, and for my expert editor friend, Liz Heaney, who asked all the right questions and reined in my humor when it got completely out of control. You're the best!

Chapter 1

If This Is So Serious, Why Am I Laughing?

My laughter started in the most curious way. I sat at the wheel of my dark red Voyager van, remembering the events of the weekend. My head ached, my eyes puffed out to my eyeglasses, and a piercing stab cut into my chest as I wound through mountain roads back to Sacramento to my parents' house after two tornado-like days with my teenagers. I was taking summer courses in Sacramento to fulfill requirements for my English teacher credentials and zipping home on the weekends.

I had been feeling pretty content. I was managing a heavy summer course load, three of my four kids were working, my older daughter had been accepted at a terrific Christian college, and my older son was having fun playing baseball in an advanced league in nearby Reno. Life had been good...until I'd arrived home two days ago, midway through the summer.

Soon after I walked through the door, I trudged from room to room, gathering my teenagers' work clothes. Rebekah labored for the U.S. Forest Service during the summers and Justin for my husband on our farm, so their clothes were reliably filthy...and reliably waiting for me on their floors. I untypically remembered to check their pockets and found in my son's jeans a small plastic cylinder with a screw top—we used it to hold matches on camping trips.

Matches? Why would he need matches?

Inside I found a cigarette. *Okay, he's experimenting. They've been out with friends a little this summer.* But I thought they knew better. I determined I'd talk to Justin about the stupidity of smoking when he got home from work—Rebekah, too, since they were hanging around with the same crowd. My husband, Craig, works late hours during the summer, so I sat down with both kids about an hour later.

Justin is six feet three with the perfect shade of red hair and a slight sprinkling of freckles—a shy young man, which is belied by his quick wit and cockiness. Rebekah is five feet seven and a half, athletic, outgoing, with rich, wavy brown hair and knock-'em-dead blue eyes. They'd made early commitments to their Christian faith and were leaders both in our church and in their school. I knew I'd instantly be able to read what they'd been up to. They were good kids. However, a few minutes into our conversation I found out they really hadn't been very good at all, and I found myself feeling rather helpless.

I had thought I knew how to handle teenage discipline problems. As a teacher I had complacently sat through hundreds of parent-teacher conferences. The most common words I'd hear were "Mrs. McHenry, I just don't know what do." And I'd judgingly think, *Well, just parent them.* But instead, I'd murmur synthetic sympathies and help set up a reward system or homework system or checkpoint system. But when my own teenagers were out of control, I found that parent-designed systems don't always work.

For the first time in my life I felt the real, physical sensation that my heart was breaking. My kids had ripped me up, and I sat there bloodied and shamed. I never thought my children would get involved with the wrong crowd. I never thought they'd smoke or drink—and to this day, I'm still not certain they haven't experimented with drugs. I never thought they'd succumb to peer pressure. But it all happened in just a year's time—six months before and after I found that cigarette. And why? My daughter summed it up, I guess, when she told me that night, "I just got tired of everyone calling me a goody-goody. I just wanted to be accepted."

So when I heard Twila Paris singing "God Is in Control!" on the car radio on the Sunday night after that rough weekend at home, it was a curious answer to my weekend-long prayer, "Lord, I don't know what to do!" As I listened to the song, I started cracking up. I still don't know why. But there I was bombing down Interstate 80, singing loudly with Twila, "GOD IS IN CONTROL!" And laughing—belly laughs. Full-bodied ripsters. The whole idea—God being in control—somehow seemed laughable. I mean, it made no sense and perfect sense both at the same time. My teenagers were out of control. While Craig and I did our best to keep them under control at home, we couldn't control what we couldn't see beyond our home and farm.

God in control? Suddenly it struck me that the only thing I could do was let God be in control. In fact, the best thing for my kids was not MY control or my husband's or even some legal authority's, but GOD'S. Somehow I knew that if I released my control to God, he would take care of the situation.

I realized at that moment on the interstate that I'd been like an umbrella for my kids their entire life. As an umbrella protects you from the rain, I'd been trying to save my kids from God's pelting storms of consequence. Parents naturally want their children not to have to experience pain or trials, and I'd weathered many of theirs in the past. But it was clearly time for me to fold up the umbrella.

I began praying that night as I've never prayed before. I let God have my teenagers. I acknowledged before him that they were his. Later that night I did this symbolically by holding out my hands with their pictures in them. I wasn't giving up on them. I was giving them up. A peace fell over me like a warm shower.

The next weekend I explained to Rebekah and Justin what I had done. I was a little nervous about that, because I thought they might interpret this as a free rein. But I was careful to make it clear that I was going to be praying for them more than ever and that God would deal with them directly as they made good or bad decisions. I watched their faces again as they took this in soberly. When I finished, we sat in silence for a while.

Then Justin said, "Mom, I've quit."

Quit? You don't "quit" when you've only smoked one cigarette, as he had earlier said. Quitting implied an addiction or at least a habit. I had never smelled cigarette smoke on his clothes.

"He has, Mom," Rebekah added.

I knew then that more had been going on with my kids than they had told me. I also knew that I didn't need all the gory details. But two things became even clearer that night as I sat and folded clothes on the living room floor. One was that God *was* in control, as evidenced already by my kids' changed attitudes. The second was that I had to keep on praying for every aspect of their lives—every challenge, every habit, every plan, every little thing.

That's what this book is about. As parents we release our teens to God's control and learn to pray specifically for their every need. Of course, we've been praying for them every day of their lives, but at this new juncture, we begin to pray more, because they're stumbling into adulthood, and although they have no idea how to go about it, they sure don't want us to tell them how. Instead, we can let them know we are praying.

I didn't say somberly, "Justin, I'm *praying* for you. You know what *that* means."

Instead, I've decided to look for joy in raising my teenagers, which is illustrated by some of the stories I'll share. But this is more than a collection of humorous anecdotes. I address twenty-one conflict areas parents typically experience with their kids—from language to grades to drugs, drinking, and smoking—and show how to trust God for the situation and how to pray God's Word specifically for the problem. The prayer at the end of each chapter, in fact, is fashioned from the Bible.

While I believe prayer is the most specific, practical thing we can do as parents, I also offer additional insights at the end of each chapter.

- "Teens Talk" offers a peek at what other real teenagers have said about the chapter's subject matter. It can be helpful to hear the perspective of other teenagers—if only to know your own kids aren't so weird.
- "God Talks" will help you discover guidance in God's Word.
- "Others Talk" contains tips gleaned from various parenting experts whose works I've read over the years.
- "You Talk" offers several openers you can use to initiate discussion with your teen on the chapter's subject. As parents, we need to learn to communicate with our teens. If they don't know what we expect and we don't know why they want what they want, problems are certain to arise. This section is designed to help you facilitate productive communication with your teen.

I pray that you will be encouraged as you fold up your umbrella and hand it over to our heavenly Father, who, after all, is the only one in control during the storms of our lives.

Chapter 2

"What Makes You Think You're Wearing That?"

CLOTHING

I'm pretty used to the fads and fashions of teenagers. After all, I teach high school, and I've seen a lot of strange stuff walk through my classroom door. In fact, when I go shopping now, I sometimes buy clothes for myself, not because I like them, but because I think my students will. Just this year, for instance, I bought an ankle-length leopard print skirt and black lace-up boots with combat heels. Now I feel like a safari hunter slinking down the school hallway jungle.

"Cool outfit, Mrs. McHenry," my students say.

I like feeling cool. So I grit my teeth and tolerate my own children's choices, because I know they want to feel cool too.

But being cool does not extend, as far as I am concerned, to overexposure. I define overexposure as more skin than should be shown to an English teacher's eye. At our school we don't allow tank and crop tops, short shorts, hip huggers, and other skimpy apparel. I agree with this, and at the beginning of every school year, I lecture each class about what the rules are and why.

One year, after I repeated the sermon for the thousandth time, Terry raised her hand. "Mrs. McHenry," she said sarcastically, "do these rules also apply to your own kids?"

"Of course," I said. My two older children, Rebekah and Justin, were a senior and junior that year.

Terry smirked. "Then why are you getting on my case when your daughter is wearing a top just like mine today?"

I gulped. I tried to fake something funny about not having dressed Rebekah that day. But Terry's point caught me off guard. Even though I taught my own daughter, I found I wasn't aware of everything she wore—and didn't wear—at school. She'd often come into my classes clad in a bulky sweatshirt or a jacket or an oversize unbuttoned shirt. Apparently she was doing that just for my benefit and shedding those clothes for other classes and activities. She had been working for the last two summers, buying her own clothes, and doing her own laundry much of the time. Or selective laundry anyway.

Reverse psychology, I thought, as I plotted my strategy about what to do. *If I show approval for what she wears, she'll stop wearing it.*

I'd learned that idea when I judged a senior project presentation once. Mary's project was called Teenage Fashion Trends. The one point that really stuck with me was her answer to my question "What makes something go out of style for teenagers?"

She said, "When your parents start wearing it—that's the killer."

So I went shopping. I found a pair of shorts that barely covered my bottom and a matching crop top that wasn't much more than a sports bra. Then I bought a jumper that didn't reach midthigh and a tank top that barely covered everything this mother of four had developed.

I wasn't surprised when Rebekah said, "Wow! Thanks, Mom," reaching for them.

"Oh, they're not for you," I said. "They're mine."

"Yours? You intend to wear this stuff?"

"Yeah, I'm going to wear the jumper thing for play practice tomorrow."

She rolled her eyes. Rolling the eyes is a kid's dead giveaway that you've made the Fatal Parental Blunder. I asked her what was the matter. "I wouldn't, Mom," she said.

"But the point is you *would*," I responded. I pointed out that she *was* wearing skimpy things and that other teachers were now wondering, as was I, what she was trying to attract.

Well, as most lectures and all reverse psychology lessons go, that dudded out. I had to let her suffer some consequences. School rules and parent rules could force her to conform, but they couldn't change her attitude about the issue. She still felt she should be able to wear what she wanted.

So I asked God to change her mind and heart, and I prayed scriptures that spoke of inner beauty and submissiveness. That's exactly what Peter's first letter addresses—the value of living a holy life through submission to authority and one another. "Your beauty should not come from outward adornment, such as braided hair and the wearing of gold jewelry and fine clothes. Instead, it should be that of your inner self, the unfading beauty of a gentle and quiet spirit, which is of great worth in God's sight" (1 Peter 3:3-4).

I began to pray Rebekah would see that her beauty was not in the latest fad or even in her body but in who she was becoming as a woman called by God. I prayed that her beauty would grow as she studied God's Word and as she allowed it to reflect through her mien and actions and speech.

The book of Revelation had an impact on how I prayed for my daughter. I read, "Let us rejoice and be glad and give him glory! For the wedding of the Lamb has come, and his bride has made herself ready. Fine linen, bright and clean, was given her to wear" (Revelation 19:7-8). A parenthetical statement follows that says fine linen stands for the righteous acts of the saints. So I began praying that Rebekah would develop a vision that God had eternal clothing planned for her, based on her faithful service to him.

In Rebekah's freshman year in college, I began to see my prayers answered. I helped her unpack her things in her dorm room, and so I saw firsthand what new things she had picked up to wear—cute but conservative tops, sweaters, jeans, long skirts. I breathed a sigh of relief and praised God as I put each item lovingly into her drawers.

Prayer for Clothing Choices
1 Peter 3:3-4; Revelation 19:7-8

Oh, Father, my child thinks that clothes are more important than what's inside. Please show my teen that beauty comes not from what one puts on or how one fixes hair or how many body parts are pierced but that it grows from the inner self, the unfading beauty of a gentle and quiet spirit, which is of great worth in your sight. And I ask that you give my child a vision of the fine linen garment and specially fashioned crown that will only fit my child. Thank you, Fashioner of every aspect of my child's being. In Jesus' name, amen.

 ## Teens Talk

"The respect you get and status you have in school is partly based on looks and clothing."—Zak, age sixteen

"This is my generation, and there are different styles."—Michael, age fourteen

 ## God Talks

1. Read 1 Samuel 16:6-13.
2. What was Samuel's impression when he met David's brother Eliab for the first time?

3. Why do you think he had that impression?
4. To what degree do you think appearance defines who your child is? who you are?
5. Write a list of five things you love about your teen's appearance—and then give thanks to God for those things.

Others Talk

Jane Nelsen and Lynn Lott suggest in *Positive Discipline for Teenagers:*
• Observe students at your teen's school. (What do they wear?)
• Look for what teens wear at the mall.
• Think about your own materialism.
• Set up a clothing allowance, and stick to it.
• Allow your teen to learn from mistakes if he or she goes over budget.
• Don't lecture or judge.
• Remind yourself that your teen won't carry the "teen look" into adulthood.
• Set up an appointment for your teen with a hairdresser or makeup specialist.[1]

You Talk

• What are your favorite outfits and why?
• Guess what I wore when I was your age. (Get out your yearbook.)
• What do you think teens will be wearing in five years?
• What do you think you will be wearing in five years?
• What guidelines do you think are reasonable for your clothing now?

Chapter 3

Car in Gear, Brain Not

DRIVING

I wasn't sure if it was a warning or a threat. But since my brother-in-law and his wife had raised three kids to adulthood, I believed it.

"When they start driving," Kenton had said, "you just have to accept that somewhere, someday, somehow they'll get in an accident. You just hope and pray it won't be serious."

Each of their three kids had been in one. None had any injuries—they all wore seat belts. Laurie slid off the road on a rainy night. Ken Jr. was hit when someone made a U-turn on a rainy night. The youngest, Sean, decided to teach himself to drive at age thirteen and rolled their topaz Escort into a ditch and through a fence. All went on to better things.

We heard these stories as our kids began their drivers' training at school. I shuddered when I thought about their starting behind the school car wheel. Frankly, I was afraid I might have passed on my Driver's Training Accident Gene to them. In fact, I earned a reputation at school for knocking down a ten-foot Cyclone fence. But it wasn't my fault! The instructor didn't tell me to keep my foot on the brake until I shifted from Drive to Park. I figured the car would stay stopped unless I did something to make it go again. But I also went on to bigger and better things too— like a van that can really plow into objects.

However, I was a little nervous when I learned that Rebekah had also set some new school records. First student to drive ON the railroad tracks, not over them. First student to play chicken with a tree. First student to take the teacher literally when he said, "Pull up to the day-care center." She jumped the sidewalk and headed for the door before he hit the brake. And so on. I was surprised to learn that she'd passed her driver's training until I realized there was NO WAY the instructor wanted to do another six hours with HER behind the wheel. He told me later, "Better your car than the school's."

Gradually, though, I gave over the keys more frequently as I learned I'd save time and gasoline by letting my teens go on their own rather than make two full trips to take and retrieve them from places.

However, I had two cardinal rules that I drilled into my kids. Number Two was Look both ways, then pray. Well, my van is always parked diagonally in our driveway in such a way that there's rarely another car on its right. So Rebekah ignored Cardinal Rule Number Two. She didn't look both ways as she backed up and swung right into my friend's red Mazda, which was parked to the right of mine. The only damage to the Mazda was a broken right headlight, but the whole left front corner of my van was smashed—I think I counted four different panels of metal.

What made me crazy was that she kept turning, rather than stopping, because "I thought I could squeeze through."

Huh? You can squeeze through crowded shopping aisles at Christmas. You can squeeze through chairs at a church potluck. You can squeeze down the rows of desks in my classroom. But a car doesn't *squeeze* through anything! The affair was a squeeze on my budget, however, when we had my friend's headlight fixed. My van stayed smashed, given our huge deductible.

Then Rebekah broke Cardinal Rule Number One: Always ask before you use the car. Her intentions were good that snowy winter Sunday at 6 A.M. She didn't want to wake us up, because she was just driving to a nearby subdivision to meet her friend to go jogging—and she thought she'd be back before we woke up.

That was the theory. The reality was that the roads were snow packed and slick. Although she was driving at a safe speed, the reality was also that another car was not, and its nonlocal driver did not see a stop sign and plowed right into the van. And so we did *not* get to sleep in that Sunday morning. The phone rang at 6:11.

"Hi, Mom."

What? "Rebekah?" I didn't remember her spending the night anywhere.

"Yeah, it's me. I've got good news and bad news."

I don't like riddles at 6:11 in the morning. "Give me the bad news first."

Well, as we know, the bad news was that she got into an accident. The good news, she said, was that she was okay and that the man's car had hit the van in the same spot she had smashed into my friend's.

"So we can get the whole mess fixed now, Mom. Isn't that great?"

I think I said something about her life being messed up when she got home. But I think this was just God's early lesson that I could not control my teenagers and their comings and goings, particularly when they're behind the wheel. But I can pray every time I know they're on the road.

I pray not only for their safety but also that they know God is in control. My children must know that it is only by his mercy that they survive from day to day. I recognize with wrenching sadness that you or someone you know may be grieving the loss of a child from an accident, illness, or suicide. I do not presume to understand your pain and do not judge you for your why questions. I ask myself sometimes, Why not my son or daughter? They're not perfect drivers. They're not perfect people. Neither am I. And so, also, Why *not* me? The only answer possible is God's unfathomable mercy. For some reason, he has been merciful to us. I pray his mercy for you.

When I pray for my children's safety, I often pray through the psalms, which speak of God as the Rescuer, the Redeemer, the Deliverer, the Shield, the Stronghold, the Protector. A special favorite is Psalm 18:1-2: "I love you, O LORD, my strength. The LORD is my rock, my fortress and my deliverer; my God is my rock, in whom I take refuge. He is my shield and the horn of my salvation, my stronghold."

When I pray, I imagine the Lord's fashioning a fortress around my child's vehicle. I mean, this thing would crumple an armored car with a single bump. It's built with granite, and the Lord's shield even replaces the windshield. And God's fortress has the horn of salvation—the most powerful honker on the freeway. All of this may sound silly, but I believe God is in control, even when my kids are behind the wheel. When I pray confidently, God reassures me of his love and mercy for my children and me.

Prayer for Driving Safety
Psalm 18:1-2

Lord, you are my strength, and I pray that you will be the perfect strength for my child as she drives. Be her rock, Lord. Form a fortress around her as she travels. Be my child's eyes and ears and sixth sense. Be her deliverer when danger approaches and provide your shield and horn when my child is not even aware she needs protection. Thank you, loving Father, that you are the stronghold in my child's life and that you continue to grant us your mercies. In Jesus' name, amen.

 Teens Talk

"I wish my parents understood that I am trustworthy. I mean, I don't go looking around for something to crash into."—Chad, age seventeen

"Last year I backed up into a teacher's truck. But my parents have had accidents too. One little fender bender doesn't mean I'm not responsible."—Cyndie, age nineteen

 ## God Talks

1. Read Psalm 46. List all of the things over which God has control, according to the psalm.
2. How is God described in this psalm? What other names for God are used?
3. What safety issues concern you about your child?
4. Write a prayer giving those areas to God.

 ## Others Talk

Gary Smalley and Greg Smalley in *Bound by Honor: Fostering a Great Relationship with Your Teen* encourage parents to have a written family contract. The following is the driving clause they negotiated:

1. Upon receiving my driver's permit, I will be allowed to drive on local errands when accompanied by either parent. I will assist in driving for extended periods of time on long family vacations under all types of driving conditions.
2. Before using the car, I will ask either Mom or Dad if I can use it and explain the purpose.
3. If I want to go somewhere for fun, both my homework and other chores must be completed first.
4. During the first month after receiving my driver's license, the radio will not be used while driving.
5. During the school year, I will be allowed to drive to activities at night but cannot take anyone home without permission. (Note:

Your state may require no youth passengers for a certain period of time after the issuance of the license.)

6. I will not allow anyone else to use the car under any circumstances without permission from my parents.

7. I will not carry more than five passengers at a time.

8. I will not give rides to hitchhikers under any circumstances, and I will use extreme caution in accepting assistance if I should have difficulty with the car.

9. I will pay half of the increase in insurance costs whenever my grades fall below a C average. In case of an accident, I will assume half of the deductible costs.

10. If I receive moving violations, I will lose my license for up to one month. On the second violation, I will lose it for up to three months.[2]

 You Talk

- If money didn't matter, what car would you buy?
- How do you feel when you drive?
- What do you think is a fair proposal about the expenses you incur for the car, including insurance, gas, and maintenance needs, such as oil and tune-ups?
- What kinds of guidelines can we set together about your use of the car?
- What kinds of maintenance helps would you like to learn so that you know how to take care of a car, such as changing the oil and fixing a flat tire?

Chapter 4

Duh...and Other Lovely Words

LANGUAGE

'll never forget the first time a student used the "f" word with me.

No, not that one.

I heard "fat."

And I murmured something about being on a perennial diet until the student said he'd given me a compliment. He meant "phat," the newest cool word for "cool."

It was the first time I'd ever appreciated being called fat.

I get quite an education as an English teacher. A lot of that education attacks me as I walk the campus. Another example occurred several years ago; I was on hall duty when I heard a student say, "That was SO bad!"

Official Righter of Wrongs, I turned around and said to the big guys behind me, "What's wrong, guys?"

They looked at each other blankly, then at me.

"Nothing's wrong, Mrs. McHenry," said one of them.

"Well, what's bad then?"

"The game last night."

I puzzled over that one. "The game? But I thought you won."

"We did. It was bad!"

It went from bad to worse until I learned that "bad" now means "good."

As an English teacher, I've taught the development of the English language to high school seniors for many years now. You know—how it changed from Old English to Middle English to Modern English. The problem is, the language keeps evolving, and this is even truer when you have teenagers in the home. I've tried to educate myself on teen lingo and actually believe I could have an intelligent—if you want to call it that—discussion with teenagers in their own "slanguage." According to a teen Web site, I could have the following conversation and be totally phat.

Me: Mark, you're not bopping Anne's work, are you?

Mark: Honda?

Me: I said, you're not looking at Anne's work and bopping it, right?

Mark: Wibble.

Me: You do too know what I'm talking about. What, is the *Beowulf* assignment too obstruse?

Mark: No, I get it. It's just nurky.

Me: Oh, bwah, you know English is supposed to be a little nurky. Otherwise, you'd enjoy it!

Mark: True. And if I work hard, I could feel systiminuous about my grade in this class for a change.

Anne: Stack-a-la-casa!

Me: Yes, Anne, I think he's stretching it a bit.

Anne: That's right, Mrs. McHenry. The yomega truth is that all Mark is good for in this class is an occasional babaloo.

Me: I thought I smelled something.[3]

My experience at home is not too different from that. I occasionally have to act like a "duh-my" when I ask my children to explain what they mean. But teen slang isn't the only language problem they bring home; so is foul language, back talk, lying, and gossip.

As a teacher, I've noticed that *foul language*—particularly when directed at someone—is usually a symptom of a person's frustration and desire to control the situation. So, for example, when things aren't going your teenage son's way, he might resort to swear words to attempt to exert control. Abusive language is meant to make you feel bad or angry—just as your son feels. It's an attempt to level the playing field. It's as though your son is saying, "You hurt me. You made me mad. Now I'll do the same to you so you know how it feels."

It's rare for a student to call me a bad name, but it has happened. When one of my high school seniors got a B on a paper instead of the A he thought he deserved, he went into a twenty-minute swearing fit. I eventually had to call 911 to get help.

Additional reasons teens may use foul language include the desire to shock or intimidate people or to make others think they're cool. Some may be so programmed to respond with cursing that it slips out unawares.

My own children's language hasn't been too bad. They've used some not-so-choice expressions, but it's not part of their all-day-long vocabulary. Nevertheless, it pains me when they cuss, because they could have heard some of it from me. I used to have a problem with bad language. I thought it was no big deal compared to smoking or using drugs, but then I realized that if God listed swearing right after not having other gods and not making idols in the Ten Commandments, it was important for me to be pure of speech. Exodus 20:7 reads, "You shall not misuse the name of the LORD Your God, for the LORD will not hold anyone guiltless who misuses his name." Swearing reveals an inner attitude.

Job could have cursed God. Satan was betting he would. However, although Job lost his ten children and all his wealth, he refused to cuss God out. From the book bearing his name, we know Job was part of a heavenly challenge. Even his wife egged him on, but instead he responded, "Shall we accept good from God, and not trouble?" (Job 2:10). This story and the many laments in the Bible can help our kids and us understand that when we are frustrated, hurt, insulted, or stripped of power, it's possible to vent in godly ways—prayer, for instance.

When my kids *back talk,* I can get even more upset, because the language is directed at me. I not only don't like the language, I don't like the feeling that my child may not respect me or care about my feelings. But I may not be helping the situation when I bark orders and tell my kids what to do; they may talk back in an effort to reverse the control of the situation. I try instead to speak to my kids with the kind of language I want them to use (Luke 6:31).

Another language problem parents sometimes need to address with their kids is *lying.* Basically, kids lie for the same reason adults do—to avoid the consequences the truth would compel.

"Did you do your homework?"

"Of course, Mom."

"Did you file that report to the chairman yesterday?"

"Of course, boss."

Our clean example as parents—while it won't always guarantee the same results with our kids—is a good place to start, along with prayer, of course.

One more issue that seems to cross generational lines is *gossip.* I've seen girls in tears at school because of what others had said about them. Teens have related false stories—gossip—of theft, cheating, and boyfriend/girlfriend exploits. It never ceases to amaze me how young people can hurt others so easily...and yet, isn't that true of adults as well? Do our kids hear us passing along unkind information about others?

My prayers, then, can begin with confession for how I may have demonstrated all kinds of wrong speech—bad and disrespectful language, lies, gossip. The good teacher always models the skill correctly for the student. Sometimes I've wondered if I'm more concerned about how my kids look to others than with how they look to God. I know I need to pray less about how my teens look or speak and more about how they are heart-wise. I need to pray that the picture they present to the world—the way they look, the way they behave, the way they speak—is one that emanates from their desire to glorify God in all ways.

In praying for our kids, we can ask that their words spring from a pure heart, because "who can bring what is pure from the impure? No one!" (Job 14:4). As speech reveals the heart, we can pray that they will learn to handle their anger in productive, not destructive ways (Ephesians 4:26). When our teens encounter abrasive personalities or situations that are unjust or challenging, we can ask the Lord to keep their whole body in check and enable them to exhibit self-controlled speech (James 3:2). We can pray that our teens and we will not misuse the name of the Lord, will honor all those in authority over us, and will not lie but always speak the truth in love (Exodus 20:7,12,16; Ephesians 4:15).

Prayer for Appropriate Language
Job 40:1-5; Psalm 51

Father, I confess that sometimes my own speech is not worthy of your ears and does not glorify you—whether it's cursing or gossip or a reflection of a critical spirit. Help my child and me figuratively to put a hand over our mouths when our words would not be pure. Create in us pure hearts, O God, and may the attitude we reflect through our speech be a result of the renewal of your spirit within us. Help us think of how our language could offend others before we speak. Remind us of your joys when we are frustrated, and help us supplant bad language with edifying speech. Help us develop a practice of praise to delight you when we approach you in prayer. May this life of praise then flow over into our daily life as we encounter challenges throughout our day. May only words that would bring you delight come from our lips. In Jesus' name, amen.

Teens Talk

"The language I use is always changing, and I'm using it more to let my feelings be known."—Samantha, age eighteen

"I wish my parents would not discipline me about language they use."—Jonathan, age sixteen

God Talks

1. Read James 3:2-12. Why is the tongue compared to a horse's bit and a ship's rudder?
2. Why is it compared with a small spark?
3. What damage can bad language, back talk, or lies do?
4. Does my language need some cleaning up? In what ways?
5. What would be a good way to change these bad habits?

Others Talk

Chicago Parent magazine interviewed Cuss Control Academy president James V. O'Connor, who had several suggestions for parents:

- Don't get angry but instead explain why cursing is inappropriate. Say, "Listen when your friends swear. How many times are they calling someone names, criticizing somebody, doing one of these negative, antisocial behaviors." Teach your kids to be more tolerant of others through their language.

- Teach your teens to be considerate of others who can hear them. Just as they wouldn't punch a stranger, they shouldn't assault them with their language.

- Since swearing is "lazy language," teach teens to use a wider, more specific vocabulary. For example, parents can direct teens to express their feelings instead of using objectionable language. Instead of swearing they can say, "I'm feeling angry" or "annoyed" or "frustrated." Friends are more likely to ask, "What's the problem?" instead of turning away.

• When a teen uses an inappropriate word, suggest others that are more appropriate and more specific. That way, they'll learn to gain others' attention, which is usually their goal in swearing.[4]

You Talk

• What kind of impression do you think I make with the language I use?
• What kind of impression do you want to make on your peers? On adults?
• Why do you think you use bad language when you do?
• What do others—teens and adults—think of people who swear?
• What kinds of spiritual consequences do you think there are for swearing, lying, or talking back to a parent?

Chapter 5

Wanted—An Amigo, Red Hair Optional

FRIENDS

The first long-term prayer I had for Justin when he started high school was that he would make one good friend. He was going to need one. After all, I was his English teacher. That was the kiss of death for potential popularity, especially in our small school. In case there was any doubt of that, my daughter had informed me: "I'll never have a boyfriend with you there walking up and down the hallways."

I figured that was a good a reason to accept the job at their school. Rebekah was a sophomore, and Justin was a freshman.

That first year was rough on me, too. You could say I was a literal target of jokes that year. Whenever I turned my back, the spitballs flew—to the ceiling, the blackboard, or even me. I'm sure I didn't help Justin win friends with spitballs in my hair.

There was one guy who seemed to delight in teasing my son. Donald apparently thought my son—with his red hair and a sprinkling of freckles —resembled a certain Mayberry star. I guess most of the harassment took place in the hall (we only have one hall in our school) or locker room, but when I heard, "Go get 'em, Opie!" yelled from the bleachers during a basketball game a couple of times, I came unglued. During a quarter break, I left the score book at the official's table, marched up to the kid in the stands, and told him to stop calling my son names or he'd regret ever taking my English class.

Well, that didn't help matters. Not only did Justin have a mom who wore spitballs; she also played mother bird against bully vultures. I have no appropriate defense, other than I didn't want my kid to have to relive verbal bashes well into adulthood.

You see, there was a girl who didn't really have any friends when she was an early teenager. Even worse, she'd suffered verbal attacks. She always was a little overweight and was crowned in her ugly ducklingness with glasses in the fifth grade, back when glasses were not cool. She always thought it strange that with her improved vision the world looked so much more beautiful…except when she looked into the mirror. The spectacles only accented her rounded face and hid her best feature.

Bullying often catches the army of self unawares. The attack is deadly. Fatty. Four-eyes. Ugly. Just a moment of infliction can cause a lifetime of pain.

The girl had no friends to defend her, nor did she have an appropriate defense, because the labels all seemed so correct. How could one deny the truth? Nearly forty years later the boys are still standing on the corner, saying those mean words to that same little girl now hidden inside the mother of four children. Just as Sandra Cisneros wrote in the story "Eleven" from her *House on Mango Street,* we are still eleven when we are twelve…or thirty or fifty.

This mother bird did not want to see her children fighting the same battle. So I began praying for good friends for my kids. In asking God for a friend for my son, I prayed for someone who would be there in thick and thin. Someone who would be a good influence on him and who could remind hallway bullies that Justin's mother taught not only freshman but also junior and senior English and that she had a very good memory.

It still makes me smile to think of how God answered that prayer—with someone who would know how it felt to be called Opie. Within a couple of months, Drew started coming around. Drew was the only other red-headed, freckled guy in Justin's graduating class. Drew was polite, diligent with schoolwork, and faithful in friendship.

It's critical to pray for our teenagers' friendships, as they will increasingly have great influence over their lives. Their friends can very well influence our children's outward reflection, such as clothing, hair styles, language, and music choices. Friends can also determine how our kids spend their time—going out for a sport or doing homework or hanging around the street corner. Friends can also affect how our kids feel about family, life goals, their faith, or themselves. Eventually, our kids may mirror their friends' choices or the other way around, depending on who has the strongest personality.

Like it or not, we parents will want to recognize that teens begin to view their friends as more important than their family. They will probably begin to care more about what their friends think than what their family thinks, and they will increasingly want to spend more time with their friends than with family. Their friends may, in fact, become family to them—their social sphere as well as their sphere of influence.

One of the strongest friendships ever recorded is David's relationship with Jonathan in 1 Samuel 18–20. In this story we can see many characteristics that we'd also want to see in our children's friendships. These two young men were in a tough spot as friends. Jonathan's father, King Saul, had become jealous of David's rising popularity, due to his prowess in battle, and he attempted to kill David. But Jonathan and David were "one in spirit" as friends, and Jonathan remained loyal to the man who would eventually replace his father on the throne (1 Samuel 18:1).

Jonathan said, "We have sworn friendship with each other in the name of the LORD" (1 Samuel 20:42). From this story we see that it's important that our teens have at least one friend who has a strong faith.

We'll also want our teens to provide moral leadership in their relationships—that they'll be the leaders like Jonathan, rather than followers under negative influences. And we'll want our kids to be good friends in return—a Jonathan to a David in need.

Now in college, Justin has developed a strong circle of friends. Every few months I'll hear another name dropped, referred to as "my good buddy." I'm grateful that the Lord heard my prayers and blessed my son with friends. I'm also grateful that the lonely girl who had none in her early teen years grew to have a large circle of friends in high school who still keep in touch.

Prayer for Good Friendships
Psalm 119:63; 1 Samuel 19:1-3; 2 Samuel 1:23

Dear Father, I ask you for at least one good friend for my child—someone who will rejoice with him, weep with him, and love him. I pray that this friend is growing in his faith and that he would be a godly influence on my child—someone who would help look out for him. It's likely my child will make a family of friends and pull away a little from his real family, but I pray he'll not become dependent on friends. Help him make right choices without bending to negative peer pressure and without needing his friends' stamp of approval. For those times when my child may be drawn to someone who would not be a good influence, may your clear discernment break through any wall of deception he may be hiding behind. Lead my child, Lord, to activities that will bring him into contact with teens who will be strong, godly friends, and remind me, Lord, that our home should be an inviting, fun hangout—a place where teens will naturally want to gather. While I cannot always protect my child from bullies and those who would otherwise demean him, I thank you that even when a friend is not around, you are my child's counselor and friend, never leaving or forsaking him. Lastly, I pray that my child will be a good friend to others—someone with a kind word, thoughtful of other people's needs, encouraging, and faithful. In Jesus' name, amen.

Teens Talk

"I wish my parents didn't feel as though I would follow my friends' tracks."—Mark, age eighteen

"My friends are not all perfect. My parents don't have to like them, but they should respect them."—Ephraim, age sixteen

God Talks

1. Read 1 Samuel 18–20. How would you describe Jonathan?
2. What sacrifices did he make in his friendship with David?
3. What benefits arose out of their friendship?
4. Make a list of characteristics you'd like to see in your child's friends, and then pray that God will develop those not only in her friends but also in her.

Others Talk

Susan Alexander Yates suggests in *And Then I Had Teenagers* that there are six gifts we parents can give our children that will help us harness peer pressure in a positive way. Void of monetary value, each gift will be costly in terms of our time and convenience. She says, however, that we'll never regret the investment.

- "Gift One: Make your home the hangout." She suggests postponing our own social life and holding off on redecorating so teens can relax. She also recommends having curfews and cleanup expectations, being an on-site presence, talking to each guest, having doors open and lights on, and staying up while they're up.

- "Gift Two: Spend time in their world." Go on school trips and to their events.
- "Gift Three: Get to know their friends." Invite them to go places with you.
- "Gift Four: Get to know the other parents."
- "Gift Five: Encourage other adult friendships." Sometimes they can hear the news better from another adult they respect.
- "Gift Six: Train them to be a good friend."[5]

You Talk

- What five or more qualities would you want in a friend?
- Do you think I have a friend like that? If so, who?
- What do you think are your best qualities as a friend?
- What do you think you could do to make a new friend or to strengthen a friendship you have?
- Is our home a good place for you and your friends to hang out? How could I make our home more inviting?

Chapter 6

Homework Is Not an Oxymoron

School Stuff

As you learned in the last chapter, I've been my children's English teacher in our small high school. Actually, at one point, I pretty much was the English department, teaching seven of the eight classes. In other years I had nodded sympathetically when my kids tried to excuse away a bad grade with, "It's not my fault. That teacher hates me!" But once I put their names in *my* grade book, they couldn't use that excuse to rationalize any underachievement in my classes. I knew better!

No, I don't single out my own kids for English torture. I punish 'em all. I torment them with all kinds of assignments—grammar, vocabulary, reading, research, writing. Worst of all, I make them think. If you can't think, you can't pass my classes.

Maybe that was the problem. My kids weren't thinking.

One night close to my bedtime (which, as you have probably already guessed, is several hours before theirs) Rebekah stormed into the kitchen, threw a book on the counter, and said, "This is the most awful book I've ever read."

"I agree." It was Dante's *Inferno*, one section of *The Divine Comedy*, a classic, allegorical, poetic work about a man's travels from hell to purgatory to paradise, standard fare for Advanced Placement students. She was reading the hell part. And it *is* awful—not the writing but the tale of suffering.

"So I don't have to read it?"

"Only if you want to drop out of Advanced Placement English."

"But it's evil."

"Yes, hell is evil."

"Then it's not godly and would be a bad influence on me."

"No, you may not like the descriptive writing, but perhaps you'll be convinced that hell is real and should be avoided at all costs." I was trying to be funny. It wasn't working.

I think our heavyweight fight went the full twelve rounds. I think I won, although I felt knocked out afterward. As a teacher, I have often found that I take students' cares and complaints home with me, but when they are actually standing there in my kitchen as well, it is doubly dismaying.

I'll admit it. Craig and I expect our kids to do the best they can, given their God-given abilities and very busy extracurricular lives. We want them to graduate and become adults…and sure, good grades would be nice also. As a little girl, Rebekah was disappointed once when she got her report card.

"They're not straight A's, Mom," she said, handing me the report card.

I looked it over. It was a beautiful report, one A after another.

"What do you mean?" I said. "It's perfect."

"But they're not *straight* A's, Mom. Teacher wrote in cursive."

Kids can be funny. But it's not funny when your teen is not understanding math or hasn't read any of *Jane Eyre* the night before the test or hasn't turned in a lab report, which is one-fourth of the class's quarter grade. And just because I was at the end of the hallway didn't mean I always knew what was going on in each of my kids' classes. Believe me, while my kids have been good students, I've also sat through conferences with teachers when things weren't too peachy.

Maybe your teen doesn't care about school at all. Maybe a learning disability frustrates his or her attempts to succeed. Maybe you're not sure your teen will cross the commencement stage.

School seemed like Public Enemy Number One to us for a few years. Details are unimportant, but we chose during that time to have our kids in a Christian school. Then we felt directed to have them in public school again. When I became a teacher myself more than thirteen years ago, I learned what it's like on the other side of the roll book, so I'll take on a few myths about teachers and school in general.

Top Ten School Myths

10. *"I don't have any homework tonight."*
Your teenagers *always* have homework, like "Read the whole textbo
tonight" or "Memorize the Constitution." There's close to 0 percent
bility that if they are taking six to eight classes, all those teachers w
what they've done in the classroom that day is enough. It's neve
we can always find more torture for your children to comp'

9. *"My teacher is an idiot."*
Your children's teachers are *not* idiots. Most te
equivalent of a college master's degree. Beside
"a feebleminded person having a mental a'
I'd say my mental age is closer to five o
teaching kids all day long.

8. *"I'll never use this stuff in real*
Not true. Educational expert.
thing we learn, we are training ou.
ics at addition and subtraction, our br.

mental faculties it could. As for me, I personally graph algebraic equations every time I balance my checkbook, which is about once every year or so.

7. "School is boring."

Every class period twenty or more different souls pile into my classroom, each with different needs and ideas and ways of expressing them. Teachers may not be too exciting, but your children can determine whether or not to be bored. In fact, your teens can be the ones to make a class interesting. For example, John had us all in hysterics a year ago when he kept reminding us odorously that he'd had three burritos for lunch.

6. "My teacher isn't fair."

We are fallible creatures and do make judgment mistakes. However, I've tried so hard to be fair that I even wrote up my own kid for detention years ago. These days teachers don't give grades; we put all the points into a computer and let the computer decide who's got an A and who's got a D. Blame it on the computer!

5. "My teacher lost my paper."

Sometimes my students' essays have spaghetti or tea stains on them, but I don't lose them. When my own children have given me this line, I tell them, "Look in one of the following: (a) your notebook, (b) your locker, (c) your room underneath the dirty clothes on the floor, or (d) your friends' rooms underneath their dirty laundry."

"My teacher embarrasses me in class."

I'm not perfect. I find it difficult to respond with grace when students whine, get angry at, or even swear at me, but I'm the teacher—not the student. I need to demonstrate self-control to the others who are intently listening. Besides, I don't want spitballs thrown at my hair as I've turned.

3. *"The work is too hard."*

This is absolutely true...when students *first* get the assignment. Otherwise we wouldn't call it "work"; we'd call it "play." Sometimes students just need to swim around in the text or ideas for a while and let the concepts sink in or get some extra help.

2. *"My teacher doesn't teach."*

Some do it better than others, and five math teachers may use five different methodologies. One of my own high school math teachers used square dance to teach geometry, and I am proud to say that not only can I now recognize a square, I can do-si-do fairly well.

1. *"My teacher hates me."*

Okay, maybe we rejoice a little bit more when some kids pomp and circumstance their way down the aisle, but we don't hate them. We'd be idiots to voluntarily go to a job every day that was swarming with teenagers if we hated them. And I think I proved we're not idiots...at least not most of us.

I've heard every excuse in the book. You know the "dog ate my homework" one? Well, I had one student tell me she couldn't read the novel, because her dog ate the book. And it did! Half the paperback was chewed away! Seriously, my own kids have used those ten excuses, and while there may have been a pinch of truth here or there, the ultimate reason for their lack of success in a class was their not taking responsibility.

I've found it's important to pray that my children take ownership for their learning. We parents can help our kids develop good organizational skills, such as using a daily assignment book. We can provide a quiet place and time for studies. We can model learning ourselves by turning off the television and reading at night. Ultimately our teens need to take ownership over their studies and the resultant grades. We can pray they will accept this responsibility and do their best.

I struggled for years with enabling my kids and bailing them out. If one of them had left an assignment home, somehow I'd figure out a way to rush back to get it on a break and save their day. Unfortunately, this does not teach them how to solve their own problems. A friend has recently taught me in those circumstances to say, "I'm sorry that you __(fill in the blank)__. What are you going to do?" I can help them think of a solution to the problem, but I do not fix it for them.

We can also pray that our kids resist the temptation to blame. It's easy to blame the teacher, the school, the system in general. Craig and I don't allow our children to complain about their teachers. For example, one of Bethany's teachers has had students with the highest grades on achievement tests in the entire state. Even though Bethany is a good student and loves and prays for her teacher, she complains at times about this teacher. As parents we'll want to cut off our children's complaints and pray that they will "do everything without complaining or arguing" (Philippians 2:14).

Instead, we can model godly encouragement and partnership by praying for our children's teachers. In Colossians 4:3, Paul asks for prayer "for us, too." Shari M. Larson, executive assistant for Moms in Touch, International, recently told me that teachers and administrators appreciate the prayers of parents. "Many have been moved to even start their own Faculty in Touch groups. Overall, we have received very positive response from the school staff and administration."[7] (If you're interested in the ministry of Moms in Touch, International, see the endnote for contact information.)

Our children will not get wisdom or an education by osmosis. They will need to take responsibility and take action. There are lots of conditions to obtaining wisdom, lots of "ifs," according to Proverbs 2. God gives wisdom, knowledge, and understanding *if* we accept his words, listen, ask for insight, and passionately pursue such knowledge. For our children to grow in understanding, we'll want to pray that they grow in recognition of their responsibility in the learning process.

Perhaps you're uncertain of your teen's potential. You can ask to have copies of standardized achievement and aptitude test scores from your child's cumulative file at the school. They can help direct you as you work with your teen to set reasonable goals, yearly schedules, and expectations about performance. Paul was a man who knew his strengths and capitalized on them (2 Corinthians 11:5-6). Once you know your teen's academic strengths and interests, you can pray that God will use your child for his perfect will.

Prayer for School Work
1 Corinthians 4:7; Proverbs 19:20; 1 Timothy 5:1; Titus 3:14

Father, I thank you for the gifts you have given my child—her special abilities, interests, and ways of expressing them. I ask you to help her teachers recognize her gifts and encourage her in her work. I pray that school representatives and I will guide her wisely in her course of study so she is moving in the center of your will. I pray that she will appreciate the uniqueness of each of her teachers, show them respect, and develop good relationships with them. Help my child have a positive attitude in all her classes and school situations and participate enthusiastically in all classroom assignments. I ask that my child will learn and incorporate study disciplines in her life to make the most of the time and talents you have given her. Help me to model learning in our home so my child understands that education is to be pursued throughout a lifetime. In Jesus' name, amen.

 ## Teens Talk

"I do the best I can, and I deserve a little credit."—Fallon, age seventeen

"I try my hardest, and sometimes the grades don't show that."—Bekau, age fourteen

God Talks

1. Read about the benefits of wisdom in Proverbs 2.
2. Make a chart with two columns. Label the first one Conditions, and list all the "if" statements from the text—what we're supposed to do. Label the second column Results, and list what God does when we follow the conditions.
3. How does God want our children—and even us—to approach the learning process?

 ## Others Talk

California's Department of Education gives tangible suggestions for parents to help their children academically:

- Talk with your children about school and everyday events.
- Read with your children, or encourage them to read for fun and discuss what they read.
- Monitor your children's television viewing, and talk with them about the programs they watch.
- Be affectionate with your children, and express interest in their school progress and their development as individuals.
- Supervise homework, making sure that your children have a place to work and that assignments are completed.
- Encourage exercise and good nutrition.
- Encourage your children to write.
- Provide learning experiences outside of school—parks, museums, libraries, zoos, historical sites, and games.
- Communicate that education is important, and encourage your children to do well in school.
- Promote good discipline—children don't know intuitively how to behave; parents must teach them.[8]

You Talk

- What is your favorite class right now? What makes it your favorite?
- What kinds of assignments do you prefer? Why do you like them?
- What one good thing do you think you will take away from each of your classes?
- Which one will help you most later—in college or at work? Why is that?
- How can I help you here at home to be more successful in school?

Chapter 7

Work Is Not a Four-Letter Word

Chores and Bedroom Messes

Generally, I have only a couple of rules regarding my kids' bedrooms. The first is that their rooms have to be clean when company comes.

The other day Joshua said, "So what you're doing is showing off the house."

"Right," I said, "and showing you off too. They wouldn't be able to find you in that room the way it's looking now."

The other rule is that the only living organisms allowed in their rooms are my kids (and their company), their pets, and their biology experiments. I have to include the biology experiments, because one year Justin did one on raising goldfish. He had one tank of ten goldfish that he kept in the light; in another tank, an exact replica, he had ten fish that he kept covered under a dark cloth all the time. At the end of the project he had— you've probably guessed—twenty dead goldfish. I tried to warn him. I say the last rites over living things like fish and plants when they enter our house to stay. They never leave alive.

The tanks came in handy when Rebekah wanted to do a project on raising snails. She could have done one on raising dust for the level of difficulty there. Here are the directions for raising snails:

1. Put snails in fishtank.
2. Watch them multiply.

That's about it. When a few hundred of them started to head for the greener pastures of her bedroom, I announced, "Project completed," and informed Rebekah that the snails had to go. Even though she'd gotten attached to the things (perhaps literally on some days), she agreed they needed to be in their natural habitat and took them to the creek.

By the way, when it came time for Joshua's science project this year, I was relieved that it didn't involve living things. He created a method for turning manure into methane gas. I knew that one was bound for success, as my kids seem to have a knack for making bad smells in their bedrooms out of natural substances. Now wouldn't it be great if we parents could turn our kids' bedroom messes into something that could solve our nation's energy crisis?

At times, however, my kids' rooms have had uninvited creatures. There've been a couple of times when I've found little wormy, crawly things thriving on the bottom layer of their messes. I need to mention that I don't regularly clean their rooms; in fact, on the rare occasion I do, I give them a bill that they can either pay or work off by doing other chores.

It's a rare teenager who keeps his or her room clean. Finding those little wormy, crawly things has convinced me that a middle-of-the-road position on teens' messy bedrooms is an arguable position. Half of the parenting books tell you to let your kids deal with the consequences they have set up for themselves. This would mean they could keep their rooms as they want—messy or not; when you have company, they advise, you just shut the door. Another group of parenting books takes a rewards or control viewpoint; they advise that you pay your children for a set list of chores weekly, with keeping a clean bedroom one of the chores. When the room is not clean, the child doesn't get paid, or you enforce other restrictions. I believe I am responsible for my child's health; kids stay healthier when a room is free of dust mites and little, wormy, crawly things—so they have to clean them at least every two weeks.

While messy bedrooms and chores in general often become a hot point of debate, they're really not major issues compared to drinking and taking drugs. Yes, I hope my kids respect Craig and me and will do what we ask them. But often our kids are busier than we are, and cleaning a room or washing the dishes may not be the highest priority at night when a term paper is due the next day. In Ecclesiastes 3:1 we learn that "there is a time for everything, and a season for every activity under heaven." Much of the passage that follows deals with work issues:

"a time to plant and a time to uproot" (verse 2)

"a time to tear down and a time to build" (verse 3)

"a time to search and a time to give up" (verse 6)

"a time to keep and a time to throw away" (verse 6)

"a time to tear and a time to mend" (verse 7)

As parents we can pray that our children—inspired by our own example—see work as an important part of life. The writer goes on to say that while God did lay the burden of work on man, he makes "everything beautiful in its time" (verses 10-11). This "beauty" comes, I think, when we find joy and satisfaction from work (verses 12-13). Is my attitude good about going to work on Monday morning? If I'm praying that my children will joyfully go about their tasks at home, then I'll have occasional attitude checks so that my life demonstrates joy about the privilege of having work—both at home and elsewhere.

Children are often end-centered as they approach a job; they're only there to get the paycheck. While we learn from Proverbs 14:23 that "all hard work brings a profit," we can pray that the greater outcome is when the job itself becomes its own reward. The writer of Ecclesiastes penned, "So I saw that there is nothing better for a man than to enjoy his work" (3:22). Finding pleasure in the now—in the tasks we do all day long in our workplace or home—is what's important. Our teens need our prayers to find purpose and contentment in the now of work—since cleaning bedrooms, doing chores, and working fast-food registers may otherwise seem like drudgery.

In regard to those bedroom messes, most of what I find in God's Word about property issues is that we've forgotten whose stuff it is. We see in Psalm 24:1-2 that "the earth is the LORD's, and everything in it, the world, and all who live in it; for he founded it upon the seas and established it upon the waters." Essentially, everything we have comes from God and is his—and yes, we are to take care of it but not make it the center of our lives. He should be at our center.

Another principle on management comes from Christ, who taught us, "Do not store up for yourselves treasures on earth, where moth and rust destroy, and where thieves break in and steal.... For where your treasure is, there your heart will be also" (Matthew 6:19,21). I often find my life filled with earthly clutter—things I don't use or never will need. A healthy practice as a family is to pray about what we choose to buy and what we choose to keep. I tell my kids, "If you haven't used it in a year, chances are you won't use it in the next one." As parents we can model this "clean and glean" method and encourage our teens to give away clothes and belongings as they acquire new ones. That practice cuts down on the mess and allows our kids to bless someone in need.

Other issues relating to chores and work are motivation and example. Just today Bethany was complaining about having to help her dad water newly planted trees on the farm. I spoke Paul's admonition to the Colossians before her as a prayer: "Whatever you do, work at it with all your heart, as working for the Lord, not for men, since you know that you will receive an inheritance from the Lord as a reward. It is the Lord Christ you are serving" (Colossians 3:23-24). We can pray that our kids understand that whatever they do, they are doing ministry if in their kindness to others (even at home, even to Mom!) Christ shines through. Their menial tasks—including cleaning their room—will then take on significance.

This concept of witness is critical. Paul also wrote that we should make it our ambition to lead a quiet life, to mind our own business, and to work with our hands so that our daily life may win the respect of others and so that we will not be dependent on anybody (1 Thessalonians 4:11-12). Whatever we do, we have a witness—good or bad. I've prayed that when my children work, they bring honor to Christ—that they'll be honest, hard-working, and reliable, among other good qualities. It was a delight at the end of last summer to get an e-mail from Justin's superior at the U.S. Geological Survey. She said she couldn't say enough about the fine job he had done—and that her boss was going to get him a job with the USGS near his college campus. That was an answer to multiple prayers!

Prayer for Bedroom Messes and Home Chores

Psalm 24:1; Matthew 6:19-21; Proverbs 22:6; Ecclesiastes 3:1; 4:7-8; Colossians 3:23-24; 1 Thessalonians 4:11-12

Father, we know that the earth and everything in it is yours. Help my child and me, then, to take care of those things you have entrusted to us. Teach us not to store up and love these things in our care but to put our energy into serving you instead. Help me to model the way in which my child should go by working with a joyful heart around the home. Thank you for providing a time for everything, including work. Show my child how to find contentment and purpose in the everyday chores he does. Help him understand that whatever he does—whatever life's pursuit he chooses—he can throw himself into his work as though it were for you, because it is you he ultimately serves. May he win the respect of outsiders—even me here at home, as he cares for his room and helps around the house—and expand the borders of the kingdom because of his admirable witness. In Jesus' name, amen.

 ## Teens Talk

"I can't stand it clean. It makes me uncomfortable."—Jessica, age sixteen

"I wish they would pay me for extreme chores."—Jonathan, age sixteen

 ## God Talks

1. Read Ecclesiastes 3:1–4:12.
2. Ecclesiastes 3:9 asks, "What does the worker gain from his toil?" What do you think we should gain from a job? What do you gain from your job?
3. What do you think is the most important benefit of work? Why?
4. What could motivate your child to do more at a job than "chasing after the wind" (Ecclesiastes 4:4)?
5. Taking care of our homes and things takes time. How can we learn to balance the time we spend on acquiring, using, and maintaining earthly things with that which is longer lasting, such as relationships?

 ## Others Talk

In *Suddenly They're 13, or, The Art of Hugging a Cactus,* David and Claudia Arp suggest the following if teens don't follow through on bedroom maintenance:

• Offer a reward. Your kids' allowance can be based on the condition of their rooms.

- Try humor. Put a note on the towel: "Hello, I don't like being on the cold floor, please take me back to the bathroom and hang me up. Thanks! Your loving towel."
- Negotiate. If your daughter's sports equipment clutters the floor, ask her if she'd keep things picked up if you got an antique trunk that could double as an equipment box.
- If nothing works, close the door. When the room becomes a major issue, a major battle may ensue—which may not be worth the relationship damage that could occur.[9]

In regard to household duties, Tricia Goyer writes in *Nashville Parent Magazine* that parents can use the following strategies to win the chore war:

- Designate a place for every item your child owns.
- Establish a weekly cleaning schedule.
- Encourage family members to work together on chores.
- Don't assume kids know how to do the job. Show them how.
- Rethink your definition of *clean*. Kids may not be able to do a chore as well as you can.
- Break down large jobs into individual tasks. "Clean your room" may sound overwhelming. "Straighten your books on this shelf" isn't so daunting.
- Counsel your children about natural consequences, such as "being late for a ball game because they cannot find their mitt in an untidy room."
- Teach your kids this phrase: "Don't put it down; put it away."
- Follow through—even when you're seemingly too tired. (I'd add: You'll be even more tired if you try to do all the work yourself!)[10]

You Talk

- What do you think is a fair arrangement about keeping your room picked up?

- If you could change things about your room, what would you do?
- Other than doing your housecleaning for you, how could I help you better organize your things?
- What kinds of chores around here do we have to do regularly, and which of those do you prefer doing?
- What do you think would be a fair distribution of chores?

Chapter 8

If There's "Nothing to Do"...
They Shouldn't Be Late

CURFEWS

We live in a town of twelve hundred folks, and there's too much to do.

My kids would argue to the contrary, but they're wrong. No, there's no Disneyland, no water-slide park, and also no arcade or movie theater. However, on any night of the week there's something to do.

When a friend of mine moved here years ago from the San Francisco Bay area, she looked across the quiet mountain valley and said, "Janet, do you ever get bored here?"

I laughed...and gave her my list. T-ball, Little League, senior league, JV and varsity baseball. Junior high volleyball. Voice lessons. Ballet lessons. Piano lessons. Guitar lessons. Flute lessons. Little league basketball, junior high basketball, JV and varsity basketball. Track team. Golf team. 4-H. Future Farmers of America. Future Business Leaders of America. Culture Club. Church youth group. Youth choir. Junior high, high school, and community plays. Recitals. Regional and state conventions. Leadership training events.

"Do you want the summer camp list?" I asked.

She shook her head and changed her question: "Do you ever have time for yourself here?"

No, I didn't.

However, if she'd asked my kids the same question, they'd have moaned, "There's nothing to do in this town."

The thing is, I read Dear Abby every day, and I know that kids in Chicago, Miami, and Los Angeles say the same thing. So the question I want those kids to answer is, Why do you stay out so late when "there's nothing to do"?

I could even guess what their answers might be.

(a) I forgot to wear my watch.

(b) I ran out of gas.

(c) I ran out of money for gas.

(d) All of the above.

(e) I was kidnapped in Reno at the mall and forced to watch dumb, dumber, and more dumber movies until I lost all my brain cells, couldn't find the car, took the wrong bus, and ended up in Yuba City. Where is Yuba City?

I'm a smart parent. I caught on. I only accepted answer "e" three times from my kids. And I KNOW where Yuba City is.

Excuses aside, curfews can create conflicts between parents and teens, but there seem to be some relevant issues that can form our prayer strategy as we approach God and talk with our teens.

Sleep requirements. The research I've read indicates that while teens average less than seven and a half hours of sleep a night, they need between nine and ten hours, because the hormones that are critical to growth and sexual maturation are released mostly during sleep.[11] When they're out late, it takes as much as two hours or more for their bodies to quiet down so as to allow sleep. Even when they're sleeping in late on weekends to catch up, they're not really, because we don't sleep as well during hours of light, according to the Sleep Disorders Center.[12] As adults we've learned how much sleep we need to function well the next day. We know what kinds of activities exhaust us and keep us from performing at our best. Teens often do not. They still need the boundaries that parents can provide; they need for us to help them frame their day. My kids often can't project that an all-nighter will wipe them out for a couple of days later. They're just focused in on the fun of the moment and don't know when to quit. As parents we can provide appropriate bedtime routines and pray our teens develop an understanding of their sleep needs.

Safety. Curfews can also protect our kids from harm. While overall violent crimes are more likely to occur during the day, about two-thirds of rapes or sexual assaults occur at night. Being close to home may not matter; 73 percent of violent crimes occur within five miles of home. Most sexual crimes are committed by someone the victim knows, while most robberies are not.[13] And teens are prime candidates for crime victimization. In 2000, young people from ages twelve to twenty-four sustained violent victimization at rates higher than those of all other ages. Sexual-crime rates are higher for kids ages sixteen to nineteen, and teens are twice as likely to be robbed as people who are twenty-five to thirty-four and ten times as likely as those age sixty-five or older.[14] I don't write this to scare you but to encourage you to provide reasonable curfew guidelines and to pray for your child's safety.

Law. Many communities have a legal curfew. I just found out that our little city's is eleven o'clock on any night of the week. Your community's curfew should be something you consider as you establish your own guidelines. To find this out, call your city clerk or police department. As legal guardians, we parents are responsible for what our kids do, and we will want to let our kids know this. If my kid tags a store window with acid, the buck will stop at my door.

Courtesy. Rather than taking a heavy hand with curfews, though, I think it's more effective to make curfews a matter of courtesy. When Craig and I go out to dinner or a movie, we let our kids know where we'll be and when we'll be home. If we're going to be later than expected, we call home. If our plans change, we call home. Teens will learn by habit to do the same when it's a common practice to keep others in the family informed and to pray for those who are on the road.

Trust. When they want to stay out late, your kids will argue, "Don't you trust me?" Of course we want to trust them, but trust is earned. If our son is a few minutes late, we don't sweat it, but if we find out he's gotten into trouble in one place when he was supposed to be at another one, trust erodes, and the curfew needs to be adjusted. I can pray that our teen will grow in responsibility and trustworthiness as he is tempted to push his curfew limits.

I liken the need of my kids for boundaries to the way the Lord led the children of Israel from Egypt to the Promised Land. During the day the Lord went ahead of them in a pillar of cloud; at night he used a pillar of fire to guide them (Exodus 13:21-22). These guides formed a frontal boundary for the Jews as they traveled through dangerous lands, and because they followed the Lord's leading, they were protected in their travels. Similarly, we'll want to help protect our kids—from their recklessness and others' harm—by providing reasonable curfew requirements and by praying for them.

Prayer for Curfew Concerns
Daniel 6:13-24; Exodus 13:21-22; Numbers 14:9; 32:17

Father, I could become frantic with many safety concerns as my child is out at night, but I will choose to trust in you, who protected Daniel as he was thrown in the lions' den and the Jews as they traveled through dangerous lands. Even when my physical protection is absent from her, I know you are there with her. Thank you for watching over my child. Lord, help me to be a consistent, disciplined influence over my child, providing routines at home that promote her health and growth. I pray that a spirit of cooperation and courtesy will embrace the way we handle these matters regarding our comings and goings—that I will show my child respect for her growing need for freedom, but also that she will demonstrate respect for me as her parent. Help us to have good communication and friendly cooperation about our plans for the day and evening. Please give me godly discernment as we discuss reasonable expectations and boundaries for curfews and sleep patterns. In Jesus' name, amen.

 ## Teens Talk

"I like being able to set my own curfew, but don't freak out if I am a few minutes late."—Fallon, age seventeen

"I completely agree with it, but if they can never trust me on my own, when will I ever learn?"—Allison, age seventeen

 ## God Talks

1. Read Exodus 13:17-22.
2. Why did God lead the Israelites in the way he did?
3. God provided boundaries for the Exodus. Without his help and direction, how might the Israelites have gotten into trouble?
4. Read Ezra 9:9.
5. For what reasons are walls and boundaries given to us? How can we communicate those truths to our teens?

 ## Others Talk

On curfews Dr. Neil I. Bernstein advises in *How to Keep Your Teenager Out of Trouble and What to Do If You Can't:*

- During the week it's reasonable to expect your teen home by dinnertime.
- On school nights she shouldn't go out after dinner without a good reason, like an errand to run, a study session, a music lesson or play practice, a school event. If these activities don't have a definite end time, assign one.
- Make sure your teen always understands exactly when you expect her home.
- School dances or games have an approximate end time, which can dictate an appropriate home arrival time.
- For weekends, vacation, and summertime, you can either assign a set curfew or assign a curfew based on the individual request. You don't have to compete with the most liberal parents in setting your rules, and it's better to err on the side of caution.
- Parents need to know where their kids will be, how they can get in touch with them, what the agreed curfew is, and if plans change. A cell phone, beeper, or phone card can help teens stay in touch.[15]

In *Teen Tips,* Tom McMahon writes that some parents set an alarm for the curfew time or leave the hall light on. The agreement is then that when the child arrives home, he can turn off the alarm or light, and when the parents awake, they know their kids are home. However, one parent has noted that, as a kid, he used to turn off the light and then sneak out again.[16] Aren't kids clever?

You Talk

- Do you feel I communicate well with you regarding when I'll be gone and where I'll be? If not, how could I improve?
- How much sleep do you think you need—and how can I help you sleep better?

- What things should you and I consider as we work out a mutually agreeable curfew?
- What would you propose for curfew guidelines for weekdays, nonschool nights, and special events?
- What kind of agreement could you and I make about how you'll let me know if you're going to be late?

Chapter 9

My Initials Are Not A.T.M.

MONEY

I take what I call a balanced approach to finances and money. With God's help, Craig and I paid off our home mortgage ten years ago. We also haven't had car payments for several years. (They didn't have banks when we bought our current jalopies.) We managed to pay cash for our daughter's wedding (tips: Use lots of tortilla chips, and become best friends with a DJ, travel agent, and so on). And I saved money so I could take a leave from my teaching job to write this book (better than taking stress leave, I figured).

But we've not always been the best guides for our kids about money. And here's my true confession, which I have to make, because my friends will probably read this book and tell you anyway on some talk show someday: I have twelve unopened checking account statements staring me right in the face as I write these words. True. I've just let them slide every month. Every month I tell myself I'm going to balance that checkbook, but every minute, it seems, there's something more pressing to do.

I'm beginning to dread that moment when it's the most pressing thing to do, so I've arranged with a high school senior, Noel, to do the banking math for me. She says she can put the whole thing on Quicken for me, and quicker'n a day the whole mess will be fixed. I'd abandon all shame in doing this, as you may imagine. The whole high school would know such things as how much I spend on Girl Scout cookies every year…that I'm a sucker for See's Candies fund-raisers…that my nails and blond highlights may not be so natural…and that my designer clothes come from Ross Dress for Less, not Macy's. I used to shop at Macy's, but then my kids went to college. I only wave at the mall now; it probably wouldn't want my ten-year-old van that's sometimes used as a farm vehicle to park there anyway.

While my financial history hasn't been sterling, I have learned one thing: God is the Provider. Craig is not the provider. I am not the provider. My *kids* certainly aren't either. But God is. My children used to see me get sick from worry over our finances; they used to hear their parents argue about money. My kids don't have to see or hear those conflicts anymore.

A changing point for me occurred during Rebekah's last year in high school. That October the parents of the ten or so seniors from our little church met with their youth group leader and prayed that God would lead each young person clearly to the right college or job and provide bountiful care for them to do just that. (I've written more about this prayer process in chapter 19.) The kids fasted and prayed, and for the next six months we all continued to pray. Rebekah was accepted by all the universities to which she applied, but by April we didn't know how we'd help her financially. Because of demands from a business and the farm, we hadn't been able to save for our kids' college education. But then the financial aid offers began to come in. Eventually she was able to attend a private Christian college on the West Coast, which was the most expensive school on her list. In fact, it was cheaper for her to go to Biola University than it would have been to go to a public university and stay with her grandma. The other kids have similar testimonies about God's grace-full care over their lives. He still is amazing me with his goodness and provision that he continues to show to those kids.

That year convinced me that the most important thing we can do as parents who are trying to teach our kids to use money wisely is to pray for them and with them. They should know we hand over in prayer the burdens we have about our financial needs, and they should know that we choose to trust God for every single detail. As is true about many of these concerns, our worries can transfer, like osmosis, from one generation to the next. A prayerful posture may be to ask God first to change us so our kids can see how prayer works. Do I need to do a better job of setting aside savings? Do I use credit cards too much? Do I tithe regularly? Do I need to pray about those issues first, before I pray for my own child about her use of money?

It's clear that God doesn't want our teens or us to worry about our basic needs. Read this valuable teaching that relates to money and God's provision:

> Therefore, I tell you, do not worry about your life, what you will
> eat or drink; or about your body, what you will wear. Is not life
> more important than food, and the body more important than
> clothes? Look at the birds of the air; they do not sow or reap or
> store away in barns, and yet your heavenly Father feeds them. Are
> you not much more valuable than they? Who of you by worrying
> can add a single hour to his life?…
>
> But seek first his kingdom and his righteousness, and all these
> things will be given to you as well. Therefore do not worry about
> tomorrow, for tomorrow will worry about itself. Each day has
> enough trouble of its own. (Matthew 6:25-27,33-34)

We can pray that our children will understand that worrying about money is futile.

Three principles about managing money are important prayer fronts— saving, tithing, and going into debt. While Paul warns against the pursuit of riches, because a focus on gaining wealth can lead one away from the faith (1 Timothy 6:9-10), it seems prudent to learn to save with a specific goal in mind, such as a car or other consumer purchase. Proverbs 13:11 teaches, "He who gathers money little by little makes it grow," and learning to wait for the little to grow into a lot develops patience in a teen's life—a rare quality! We can help build Christian character in our kids by modeling a practice of savings and by praying for and teaching them about saving toward a goal. Craig and I didn't do such a good job in this arena with our older two kids, but now our younger two kids have savings accounts, and I helped Josh start a checking account last summer. His work earnings are going to be used for a car he'll get after high school graduation.

Debt is challenging for all of us—teens and parents alike. While some teach that one should never go into debt and trust God instead for the need, I think Scripture shows us God's grace in this area. Romans 13:8 teaches, "Let no debt remain outstanding, except the continuing debt to love one another, for he who loves his fellowman has fulfilled the law." We see grace in this verse in the word *remain*. It implies that sometimes debt is unavoidable—a mortgage, a car loan, a large medical bill. We can pray that both our teens and we can avoid debt whenever possible and work diligently to pay back debt quickly.

Because God is the Provider, the money is really his. We know this, because "every good and perfect gift is from above" (James 1:17). We'll want to pray, then, that our teens develop attitudes and practices of appreciation and generosity as they begin to manage money. Tithing—giving 10 percent or more—to God's ministry on earth is an opportunity for our kids to learn God's provision. In urging his people to tithe, God said, "Test me in this…and see if I will not throw open the floodgates of heaven and pour out so much blessing that you will not have room enough for it" (Malachi 3:10). Through prayer and example, I can expect that my children will be obedient in this act of appreciation. Even more, I can pray that they will not just give out of duty but be generous with what God has entrusted them—not only in ministry but also toward their friends and those in need.

We can also pray that they see that the purposeful, godly pursuit of life—rather than wealth—leads to contentment. I've taken informal surveys in my classroom and also observed what teens say to career counselors. They want to be rich—filthy rich. They want hot cars, big houses, huge bank accounts. So who wants to be a millionaire? Teens do. The problem is, as the writer of Ecclesiastes said, those who love money never have enough and are never satisfied (5:10). It's still true today that as people accumulate wealth, its trappings bring a decreasing sense of contentment. Bigger is not better, but our teens think it is.

We'll want to pray they'll be seekers of God, not earthly riches, because we know that "no one can serve two masters. Either he will hate the one and love the other, or he will be devoted to the one and despise the other. You cannot serve both God and Money" (Matthew 6:24). Notice that *Money* is capitalized. Many kids view money as a god, something to make as one's life search and purpose and source of contentment. We parents will want to speak against that lie and pray that God will guide our kids' financial focus. After all, Judas betrayed Christ for money—and committed suicide when he realized his folly (Matthew 27:1-10). Praying for right attitudes about money is critical, as the Enemy can use money issues to ruin marriages and businesses and bring on illness and even suicide. Instead of letting our kids find out that "the love of money is a root of all kinds of evil," we can pray that they'll find "godliness with contentment is great gain" (1 Timothy 6:10,6).

Prayer for Right Attitudes About Money
Matthew 6:24-25; Malachi 3:10

Father, we know from your Word that no one can serve two masters—we cannot serve both you and money. Place in my child's heart a deep, deep desire to serve you. Help him pursue the riches that money cannot buy—

love, joy, service, godly contentment. In that pursuit, Lord, I pray that he will clearly see your providential care over the years, that his faith and trust in you will grow, and that he will not worry about financial obligations but make plans with your direction. I thank you and praise you for all you have given my family and me over the years. Guide my child as he makes lifelong decisions about savings and debt. Create a grateful and generous heart in him—one that lovingly gives back to you a portion of what you have given him and compassionately gives to those in need—and let him, Lord, see your floodgates of blessings pour over him. And keep me, as well, mindful of your gracious provision. In Jesus' name, amen.

 ## Teens Talk

"I work to get money for myself."—Brett, age eighteen

"I appreciate the help I get to pay for my basketball habits, even though I use the money from my job, too."—Jasmina, age eighteen

 ## God Talks

1. Read Matthew 6:25-34 and 1 Timothy 6:6-10.
2. Some people say that money buys happiness, but the Timothy passage says the opposite. What is a godly perspective about money?
3. In what ways has God provided for you?
4. What should be a Christian's plan for tithing and other giving? (Malachi 3:8-10 and Matthew 19:16-30 provide guidance.)

 ## Others Talk

Jane Nelsen and Lynn Lott suggest the following in *Positive Discipline for Teenagers:*

- Pay for work you would hire someone else to do—paying only after the work is done.
- Start your teen on an allowance that is not connected to chores. (You can include money you would give for school lunches, ball game admissions, and clothes and then allow your teen to make decisions about how to spend the money.)
- Avoid bailouts. (If they blow all their money on junk food, for example, don't give them more money to go to a movie.)
- If you make loans, start with small amounts and keep a payment ledger to track repayments. Do not lend larger amounts until the teen's credit worthiness is established.
- Teach your teen how to make a budget.
- Show your teen or have your teen show you how to use computer-based budgeting programs.
- Start your teen on a clothing allowance.
- Teach your teen tricks for saving, such as how to use an envelope system.[17]

Additionally, Janet Bodnar, otherwise known as columnist Dr. Tightwad, suggests that parents help their kids decide what portion of their income should be put into savings and help teens minimize their withholding in summer jobs, as they usually don't make enough to trigger an income-tax obligation. She also suggests parents help their kids set up a checking account.[18]

 You Talk

- What needs for money do you have?
- Which of those are needs, and which are really wants? How do you think I'd view them?
- Which of those do you think I should be responsible for, and which do you think you should assume?

- Is there something long-term for which you'd like to save? If so, would you like my help in that?
- How do you feel about tithing?
- What do you think would be a good tithing plan?

Chapter 10

"No, I Don't Want to See Your..."

Piercings, Tattoos, Dyed Hair, and Other Body Decorations

When Justin was in junior high, I committed a major sin. I allowed him to get lines in his haircut without consulting Craig. It was a popular style at the time—zigzags and other decorative designs buzzed into a boy's butch. Hair grows back, so I thought it a rather innocuous way to express oneself.

Craig did not, however. I'll never forget his reaction: "Take him back, and have the lines taken out."

Taken out? But, but…taking the lines out would mean my son would virtually be red-headed bald!

Even so, I took Justin back, and the barber took out the lines. It was okay though. Justin had hair that looked seminormal in a year or so.

I had forgotten I was married to a man who, if he had his druthers, would be married to a woman whose hair stretched to the Nevada state line. He moans every time I get my hair cut.

As the haircut story has been passed around innumerable times, you can imagine that tattoos haven't been much of an issue in our house. I think the kids figured that Dad's line—"Take 'em out"—would be much more painful for a tattoo than a hair style.

Craig has loosened up a bit as the years have gone by, though. Last year it took him awhile even to notice when Bethany got her ears pierced as a present for her ninth birthday from her older sister. Even then, I think all he said was, "You want holes in your ears?"

Bethany said, "No, Dad, I want earrings." She has her mother's wit.

I'll never forget the dramatic day I took Rebekah to get her ears pierced. It was the summer before her freshman year in high school. Most of her friends had had their ears pierced for years. It wasn't that Craig and I had been postponing the event. Rebekah has just never done well with objects that invade her body.

The first time she had a glaucoma test, I told the eye doctor, "You might want to lay her down. She faints with this kind of thing."

He chuckled and did the test, saying, "Oh, I've NEVER had that happen before."

I looked at Rebekah. "Well, it's happening now."

It was. She was fainting.

When she had her tonsils removed, of course the anesthesiologist had to insert an IV.

I said, "You might want to lay her down. She faints with this kind of thing."

Again the doctor chuckled and put in the IV, saying, "Oh, I've NEVER had that happen before."

I looked at my daughter. "Well, it's happening now."

Again, she was fainting, right there on the gurney.

I knew all this because of her early history with shots and because of the ear piercing day.

We strolled into one of those stores with a million earrings on the walls and racks, and Rebekah sat down on the high stool next to the cash register.

"Does it hurt, Mom?" she said.

I, who had waited until the eve of my fortieth birthday before getting my ears pierced, weighed my words carefully. "Um, only for about a year…or two." You see, all my friends had lied to me when they said it didn't hurt.

But before she could lift her chin, BAM! BAM! The two employees had almost simultaneously pierced her ears. I turned to sign a statement releasing those employees, the store, and its parent corporation from all liability should my child get gangrene and need to have her ears amputated, lose her hearing, die, or suffer some worse consequence. But just as I was signing, all of a sudden store fixtures started falling, and millions of earrings began flying all over the place.

I turned to find the reason and found my daughter lying on the floor. Yup. She had fainted. I looked at the form again. It didn't say anything about fainting, so I finished signing the release.

I'm just kidding. I picked up my dear daughter, who was not bleeding from those newly pierced ears but was from a few other places. I helped her sit up and remember what city and state we were in, and after a few more minutes of filling out other forms promising not to sue anyone, we left for home.

Just for the record, her ears did not turn gangrenous. Rebekah waited until college before she had another piercing done. As I recall, she was very proud of the fact that she could remember she was in Los Angeles after she fainted that time. The first time she thought she was in Yuba City.

Kids dye their hair blue and get body piercings and tattoos in the strangest places for the same reason their parents dyed, ratted, and permed—to create one of two opposite visual labels: "I'm different" or "I'm the same." They want either to be unique or to fit in with "everyone else" they think is doing the same. As we parents pray, then, a good place to start might be to pray that our teens feel good about who they are in Christ—"his treasured possession" (Deuteronomy 26:18), each special, each valued, each accepted by Christ.

A *Focus on the Family Magazine* article about piercings and tattoos lists several questions that we can discuss with our kids as they begin to voice their desires. The first is, *Is it harmful?*[19] Serious medical problems can develop from tattooing and all kinds of piercings, and until our kids are eighteen, we can say no if we feel such procedures could create health problems (see the U.S. Food and Drug Administration's statements at the end of this chapter). We can pray our children understand that we are ultimately responsible for their health as long as they are under our care and that we want them to be "vigorous and healthy" and to have long lives (Psalm 128:3, TLB).

Another question to consider is, *Is it permanent?* Most kinds of body piercings (except those in the tongue) will close up once the stud is removed, but they leave scars. Infections, which are common, can make the scars worse. Tattoos, of course, are permanent, painful, and costly to remove, also with potential scarring. What is cool today may not be tomorrow, so we can pray that our children will see the wisdom of looking ahead. Having "Jamie" tattooed on a forearm may not be too appealing to the next girlfriend.

A third question is, *Is there a rule or law against it?* Your teen's school may have a dress code that addresses piercings, hair color, and tattoos. It may be okay with you if your son pierces his lip, but it may not be with the school. Even though your teen's school may not have a rule, a certain hair color or type of tattoo or piercing may identify your child with a neighborhood gang, which would not be desirable. Some teens want to do something different as a form of rebellion, and while there's nothing wrong with creative dress or appearance in itself, we'll want to pray that our kids' hearts are turned toward us as parents rather than against us. They may not be happy with our decision to protect them in this way, but we can pray that they will honor us and the decisions we make (Exodus 20:12).

Finally, we can ask, *Could it be misinterpreted?* Kids may not be aware of the message certain "body decorations" can send. Greg Warner, editor of

FaithWorks, a lifestyle magazine for Christians committed to engaging the post-Christian, postmodern culture, quotes one source who acknowledges that "many piercings carry sexual connotations."[20] While some teens just want to do something different, their friends may associate certain types of piercings with sex. For example, even in my small high school of fewer than two hundred teens, I've heard boys publicly tease girls, in a sexual context, about their tongue piercings. You will probably want to discuss with your teen the perceptions others may draw from their "body decorations."

If your child is still living at home and receiving the benefit of your support, you can make the decisions about what forms of body art are acceptable. You may decide it's not worth the division the argument can create, but prayer can affect our children's thinking, and so we can pray not that they think like us but that they begin to have the mind of Christ in these personal decisions. In prayer, we "make it our goal to please him, whether we are at home in the body or away from it" (2 Corinthians 5:9). It pleases God to know his name is on our hearts—not necessarily on our ankle or back. I, who am known for writing things on my palm so I don't forget, find it delightful that the Lord has engraved my name on the palms of his hands; I like knowing he has also sealed our relationship forever (Isaiah 49:16).

Prayer for Deciding About Body Adornment

Isaiah 49:16; 44:5; 2 Corinthians 5:9; 1 Corinthians 15:10

Father, thank you for engraving the names of my child and me on the palms of your hands—for showing that who we are in Christ is pleasurable to you. Lord, your Word says, "One will say, 'I belong to the LORD'; another will call himself by the name of Jacob; still another will write on his hand, 'The

LORD's,' and will take the name Israel." May the most important mark we put on ourselves be "the Lord's," and may my child take joy in pleasing you with her body, personality, attitudes, actions, and everything that makes up who she is. Father, rebelliousness sometimes may be at the root of a child's appearance, but I pray that no such rebellion will ever take root in my child. May she honor my wishes, and may I, as her parent, be worthy of my child's honor. I pray that my child will make it her goal to please you in her dress or body adornment, whether she is at home or away from home. Lord, your Word says that by the grace of God we are what we are. Thank you for creating my child exactly as she is, and I pray that she will be content with the ways you have graced her. In Jesus' name, amen.

 ## Teens Talk

"I love my natural hair color but would like a change. I would also love a belly button piercing."—Mary, age eighteen

"I might joke about getting a tattoo, but I really don't mean it."—Ephraim, age sixteen

 ## God Talks

1. Read 1 Peter 3:3-4.
2. List some of the various ways we alter or adorn our bodies in an attempt to make ourselves more attractive.
3. Verse 4 says unfading beauty comes from the inner self. What would be some inner qualities that would make us beautiful?
4. What practices could we use regularly to enhance that inner beauty?
5. Pray now about those changes you feel God would have you make.

Others Talk

According to the U.S. Food and Drug Administration, you and your teen should be aware of the following in regard to tattoos:

- Tattoos and permanent makeup can result in infection, including hepatitis and HIV.
- Even laser removal is painful and expensive.
- Some have allergic reactions to tattoo pigments.
- Nodules can form around the tattoo.
- Keloids, scars that grow beyond normal boundaries, can develop.
- Some people with tattoos have burning or swelling problems when having an MRI (magnetic resonance imaging).
- The FDA does not regulate or investigate those who practice tattooing and suggests that consumers carefully choose a reputable business.

Other good advice comes from Neil I. Bernstein in *How to Keep Your Teenager Out of Trouble*:

1. Make sure your child is aware of all the possible things that can go wrong after a tattoo or body piercing. Here's a list of the most common complications:

   - The tongue swells tremendously when it's pierced. And a tongue piercing may result in slurred speech.
   - Dentists report that tongue studs can cause problems in the mouth, such as chipped teeth.
   - A pierced navel can take up to twelve months to heal, and there's always a risk of infection.
   - The health risks of piercing include hepatitis B and tetanus as well as skin reactions that can occur with red and yellow dyes.
   - According to dermatologists, removing most tattoos takes several painful laser sessions and costs between eight hundred and sixteen hundred dollars.

2. Ask your teen to wait at least a month before following through with such a decision.

3. Make a deal where your child has to wear a temporary tattoo or faux piercing first.

4. Remind your teen that some people make judgments, both positive and negative, based on tattoos and piercings, and that he or she should take that into account.

5. Warn your child that if he or she gets a serious infection from a piercing because directions weren't followed, the ring or stud will be coming out.

NOTE: If your teen seems angry, depressed, or unhappy, then you should be aware that something more may be going on, whether it's substance abuse, sexual promiscuity, clinical depression, or violent, illegal, or risk-taking behavior.[21]

 You Talk

- How do you feel about tattoos (or piercings)? Why do you feel this way?
- Which of your friends have them, and why do you think they do?
- What kinds of designs (or piercings) are the most popular?
- What groups of people do you think might change their opinion of you if you were to get a tattoo (or piercing)?
- How would that make you feel?

Chapter 11

Déjà Vu: "You Call That…?"

MUSIC

Rebekah and her college roommate are convinced they know why the university paired them up more than four years ago. They were probably the only two in all the girls' dorms who both checked on their questionnaire that they liked country music. That mutual preference cemented their relationship right off.

I wasn't sure how Ozzie would feel about country though. Ozvaldo Heredia Perez is our new son-in-law, and rap was more his style when he met Rebekah. In fact, when he found out she was a country girl, he announced she'd never see him in a pair of Wranglers.

We knew it was love when we saw the engagement video. Rebekah's girlfriends had taken her to a restaurant that had a karaoke stage. As they were finishing dinner, in walked Ozzie's friends with two dozen yellow roses. As she was trying to piece that odd coincidence together, the karaoke announcer said she had a special guest—Ozzie, dressed in Wranglers, a western shirt, cowboy boots, and a Stetson. He took the mic and sang "Amazed," the big Lone Star hit of a few years ago. Then he got down on one knee and proposed. Sigh. How could a girl say no to a guy who'd made a complete fool of himself for her?

Rebekah can croon Patsy Cline or Loretta Lynn tunes right along with the best of them. So can Bethany, who's just turning ten. Their father encourages this. He cannot carry a tune and cannot pat out a beat, but he's been a country fan for years. He even bought Bethany a karaoke player a couple of years ago. She now is "crazy" about her dad and "stands by her man" when I ask them to turn the twang down a few notches. Craig has even invested in recording equipment and has our girls on their own CDs.

I've noticed that music can have an effect on kids. My kids want pickup trucks, big dogs—several of them—and meat and taters on their plate for supper—and those are the girls!

My guys are more like Beach Boys types. They want to "round, round, get around" with a "surfer girl" in a "little Deuce coupe." And "God only knows," "wouldn't it be nice" if the car DIDN'T "shut down" just a few miles down the road.

Seriously, I think Beach Boys' songs are fun, especially if you like your lyrics simple, like "ba, ba ba, ba ba ba ba, ba ba ba, ba ba BA!" When I sing a solo, I'm known for forgetting the words, so sometimes I write them on my fingers. Verse one lyrics on the first finger and so on. Beach Boys' songs of the ba-ba variety I can usually remember, however.

Two years ago I made a fool of myself dancing all the way through one of their outdoor concerts during Hot August Nights in Reno. The "boys" are now grandpas. Even so, beachballs were flying, and a lot of midlife folks were having fun living a night of reminiscences, including Craig and me.

Most of the time our kids and we have been pretty music compatible. However, I was concerned years ago when I saw some of my son's CD jackets. They were ugly and dark, and the lyrics weren't printed on the CD cover. I told Justin I wanted to listen to them.

He said, "I don't think you want to do that."

I said, "Would you rather just get rid of them yourself?"

He culled his collection and said I could listen to any of what was left.

Our kids' music choices may not seem like life-or-death issues, but music has driven some teens to destructive, even homicidal, behavior. Over the years I've read the newspaper reports of young people who have decided to follow Satan, hurt animals, rape and even murder others, all because the music they listened to urged them to do so. I've talked to my teens and others and know what teens will say when asked why they listen to lyrics that are vulgar or suggestive: "I don't really pay attention to the words. I just like the overall sound. It helps me relax."

I used to say the same thing as a teen and young adult. But as I think back on those years, I recognize now that those lyrics may have helped to form the depression that began to seep into my soul. Many times from my early adult years until just a few years ago, I wanted to die. (My depression disappeared when I started prayerwalking.) Perhaps some of those feelings were a result of years of listening to music that was melancholy if not self-oriented, destructive, and depressing.

Christ said, "Out of the overflow of the heart the mouth speaks. The good man brings good things out of the good stored up in him, and the evil man brings evil things out of the evil stored up in him.... For by your words you will be acquitted, and by your words you will be condemned" (Matthew 12:34-35,37). Music does influence our heart attitudes and overall mood, and the words we hear and sing ourselves will come out in our speech.

I have found this true in my own life. After a hard week I was recently feeling blue when I sat down on the living room floor to fold laundry. Before I tackle that chore, I always put on Christian CDs or reflective music, and sure enough, after just a few Christian songs, my mood completely changed, and I began singing. If our kids start cussing or become depressed, a prudent practice as parents, then, would be to check out the lyrics on their CDs. Music can spark or help fuel depression or anger.

Again, you can set boundaries for your kids' music. You can decide what kind of music you'll permit in your home, whether it's played out loud or with headphones. The music will influence the mood of your home, whether or not it's heard by everyone else, because the music will influence your kids. Their anger or depression—or optimism and joy—will permeate your home. Speak against any negative influences that music could have on your teens. Pray that they will desire music that glorifies God and encourages them rather than discourages them.

Music not only influences our mood, it also reflects who we are, and teenagers know that music is part of their image. To be cool, you have to listen to music that's considered cool. I've heard kids say, "You listen to THAT?" Their peers will be the largest influence on what kind of music a teen buys and listens to, along with the attention the media gives music personalities. Our teens may also be influenced by today's culture that prescribes, "If it feels good, it is good." We know that's wrong, but teens will buy into the pressure of their culture, because they want to "be like the nations, like the peoples of the world, who serve wood and stone" (Ezekiel 20:32). It's important to pray, then, that our kids are confident enough in their own faith and good choices to withstand peers who would pressure them to listen to negative music.

Can we expect that Christian teens will be drawn to praise music for their regular musical diet? I think it's unreasonable to presume that everything a teen listens to will be upbeat and happy. Even most of the psalms, which were used for worship liturgy, are laments. Teenagers want music that sounds like their own, and wise parents will help them find and buy music that appeals to them. When I worked recently on a teen product, I was asked to find Christian musicians to endorse it. Frankly, I knew a few artists' names, but I wasn't sure what groups my classroom kids would recognize and approve of. So I asked them randomly, both Christian and non-Christian kids. When I told one non-Christian boy I was seeking a certain Christian group's endorsement, he was impressed. There are Christian groups who don't compromise their message and are accepted by mainstream kids. They'll change from season to season, so I won't mention them here, but you can find them by going to a good Christian bookstore and seeking out a teenage clerk to help. Then pray that the message will not only sink into your kid but into his or her friends as well.

This is a critical issue, because whether it's godly or not, music can form a teen's worship. Jesus said, "Where your treasure is, there your heart will be also" (Matthew 6:21). Some kids love their music so much, they can't live without it. Music is important to our spiritual development, so much so that David even put men in charge of music centuries ago, just as he put others in charge of protection (1 Chronicles 6:31-32). Our prayers can ask God that our children will worship him with gladness with their music—and not just on Sunday (Psalm 100:2).

Prayer for Good Music Choices
Psalms 100:2-3; 119:54; Matthew 6:21

Father, thank you for the gift of music—for the privilege of coming before you with joyful songs. Lord, help my child remember that you made him, that he is yours, and that you have created us to worship you. It is my desire that you will be so often on the mind and heart of my child that his musical choices will naturally turn toward those things that glorify you. When he turns to music that bears the world's influence and not yours, I ask you to lead him and me to music that meets the deepest desires of my child's heart. May your Word be the theme of his music and of his life's song. Give me insight as I make decisions about boundaries for music in our home—what is acceptable and what is not. Help us all, Lord, to make you our greatest treasure so the song of our heart draws others to you. In Jesus' name, amen.

Teens Talk

"I like my parents' music, because I grew up with it, but I need something of my own, especially through trying out new things."—Allison, age seventeen

"The music I like has meaning to me, and that is why I listen to it."—Brett, age eighteen

 ## God Talks

1. Read Psalms 100 and 102.
2. If these were put to music today, which would be your favorite? Why?
3. Which do you think your teenager would prefer? Why?
4. What elements in Psalm 102 are echoed in teens' music today?
5. Write the lyrics for a song that reflects your confidence in your child and his or her choices and future and give them to your child as a gift.

 ## Others Talk

Jerry Melchisedeck suggests in *Lyrics Don't Matter* that teens ask these questions about their music:

- Do the lyrics promote premarital sex? lust? unfaithfulness or adultery? homosexuality? violence? drug or alcohol abuse? foul language? hatred toward others? illegal activity? demonic activity? worship of something or someone other than God? doubt in God or blasphemy of God?
- Does the message increase my desire for violence, drugs, or sex?

- Does the message draw me closer to God or pull me away from him?
- Do the lyrics dwell on feelings of hopelessness and depression or promote suicide as a solution to life's problems?
- Do the lyrics promote conceit, selfishness, greed, and immediate gratification?
- Do the lyrics encourage me to think critically and make wise decisions?
- Would I feel I had to hide this music from my parents?
- Do the artist's lyrics and lifestyle measure up to biblical standards? Is he or she a good role model for me?
- Do I believe Jesus would listen to this musical selection?[22]

You Talk

- What music of mine do you like?
- Which of your CDs do you think I'd like? Why?
- How important is your music to you?
- In what way is it a reflection of you?
- What standards do you think are appropriate for music that's played in our home?

Chapter 12

A Phone Is Not a Body Part

TELEPHONE USE

I can always tell when my kids are home: The phone is missing. That's why I'm thankful someone thought of the paging device. Often, however, it takes two people to find the thing, as you must know, and so sometimes I'm beeping and running the twenty-five-yard dash around the house, trying to find the phone. Press, run, *beep, beep*. Press, run, *beep, beep*. Over and over again until I can locate it.

I've found our phone in a number of crazy places—under my daughter's pillow, in my son's laundry hamper, in a bathroom drawer, and in a pizza delivery box—in the trash, no less.

Can you just imagine this conversation between two garbage pickup guys as I was trying the paging device?

Guy 1:   George, I think the trash is beeping.

Guy 2:   Trash doesn't beep, Fred.

Guy 1:   I think it's coming from that pizza box right there.

Guy 2:   I told you Gino's Pizza was *beep* good.

Guy 1:   Well, maybe there's some left. Let's check it out.

Guy 2:   Nah, it's only another phone. What's that…ten phones this week?

Guy 1:   Nope, eleven. The Stevenses' trash had number ten.

Guy 2:   I believe you're right. Ten pagers. Eleven phones. About one per house of teenagers this week, right? I do believe we've got enough now to run AT&T out of business.

I don't think that's possible though. I'm running into the phone store about once a month to replace some device or another. Once my daughter called from Los Angeles.

"Um, Mom, I hate to tell you what I found in my suitcase when I got back to school."

"The phone?"

"Gee, how'd you know?"

I told her I just knew. After all, it wasn't in the bathroom drawer, the hamper, or the kitchen trash, so it had to be in her suitcase. Well, at least we saved on a week's worth of phone calls until the phone arrived in the mail.

My contention is that all these new devices—pagers, cell phones, phone message recorders, you name it—are making us less communicative...or worse, anticommunicative.

One example was a series of messages left on our answering machine a couple of days ago. Each of the four of us at home has his or her own line, so you, yes, "Press one for Craig, two for Janet, etc." I thought that would save someone—ME!—time, but as it works out, no one checks the machine except me.

When Rebekah lived at home, Craig and I swore we'd forgotten how she looked without the phone attached to her left shoulder and ear. She had even mastered the art of getting dressed with the thing. Once, though, when she was cheerleading in her mascot outfit, I noticed that the phone bounced on the gym floor out of her bear paw during a basketball game when we were "giving her an L."

She was lucky, however. Crystal was still on the line, and I don't think Rebekah missed a letter.

In fact, I do believe Crystal answered the question, "What's that spell?" from her side of the conversation:

"LOYALTON!"

Nowadays we have two phone lines at home—the second one for the Internet. When I want to get my kids' attention, I can plug a phone into the Internet line and call my other number.

The kids run to the phone, and then I've got their undivided attention.

"Hello! This is your mother calling. I'm just reminding you to mow the lawn and take the trash out… What do you mean you have homework and don't have time? You just spent an hour on the phone!"

This self-orientation of teens—thinking the world and family life revolve around them and their concerns—partly explains their overuse and domination of the phone. Also, as they transfer importance from family to friends, they seek out and develop these new relationships. These new "family" members become all-important, and our kids may feel the need to share with them every life detail, feeling, and upcoming concern. One psychologist writes that teens simply use the telephone for different reasons than adults use it. "Why would a fourteen-year-old girl, for example, come home from a school dance and immediately call her friends (who all had been to the same dance) to recount in great detail what had happened less than an hour before?"[23] We can pray that our teens will expand the boundaries of our family to include their friends and that, instead of replacing us with their friends, they'll bring friends into the family picture.

Josh is doing that now. Every weekday he and his four friends each drive their cars the few short blocks to our house from school to eat their lunches at our house. Craig and I not only approve of this; we encourage it by letting his friends help themselves to our kitchen cupboards. As a result, our "family" is expanding by the daily half-hour addition of these four great guys. Why not expand our boundaries a bit to demonstrate the love of Christ, even if that means giving up some of our time with our kids?

In their quest for special relationships and intimacy, teens are discovering who they are and are learning to communicate. The telephone provides this intimacy and yet privacy at the same time, as they don't have to talk face to face with someone. The phone also facilitates their need to discuss their growing ability to weigh abstract issues. Teens do not share our perspective that time will pass without the sharing of every life tidbit. Their communication with their friends is critical to them, and while we don't have to allow our kids to dominate the phone, we at least can understand this need.

Providing boundaries for phone use can serve several purposes. It can help develop our teen's awareness and consideration of other people's needs beside his or her own. It can help our child develop personal responsibility and time management skills. It can provide time for our teen to be with the family.

Some teens are naturally thoughtful. Some learn by observing positive examples. Others need reminders, such as we find in Scripture. From it we learn not to hoard things for our own use (Proverbs 11:26), to be generous (Matthew 5:42), to cooperate with one another harmoniously (Psalm 133:1), and to listen to those who are in authority with a peaceful, obedient, and considerate spirit (Titus 3:1-2). Our prayers for our teens, then, can ask God for these characteristics so that the whole household might live in a spirit of thoughtfulness and cooperation.

Prayer for Telephone Use
Psalm 133:1; Proverbs 11:26; Matthew 5:42; Titus 3:1-2

Lord, I pray that we can live in unity in our home, each person having an attitude of service toward the others rather than an air of selfishness. May each of us be a blessing to the others, and not a curse, sharing the telephone and all other facilities under this roof. Help my teen learn how to put the needs of others ahead of her own not only by giving to others in the family but by learning to anticipate their needs, offering things even before the need is made known. I also ask that my teenager will not live according to her inborn, sinful nature but according to the mind of the Spirit. Finally, I ask that my child will become peaceable and considerate, showing humility to others in the family, especially in using the telephone. In Jesus' name, amen.

 ## Teens Talk

"Sometimes I have a friend I must talk to, and my parents need to be patient."—Jessica, age sixteen

"I wish they would allow me to make my own time limit."—Jonathan, age sixteen

 ## God Talks

1. Read Luke 14:7-11.
2. What does Christ teach in this passage about having consideration for others?
3. How could this apply to the use of the telephone?
4. In what ways have we been considerate of each other in our home lately?
5. How can putting others first develop Christlike characteristics?

 ## Others Talk

Harvard Medical School faculty member and magazine columnist Lawrence Kutner suggests several guidelines regarding adolescents' phone use:

- Help teenagers understand that telephone use is a privilege, not a right.
- Make phone use contingent upon certain behaviors, such as finishing chores.

- Set limits on lengths of calls and hours for telephone use.
- Consider getting a second phone line, especially if there are several teens in the house.
- Also, with a separate line, set up clear rules for its use. For example, don't allow teens to call on the parents' line if the teens' line is busy.
- Set up a system for paying the phone bill, especially long-distance charges—helping teens ease into autonomy for when they'll leave home.[24]

You Talk

- Do you think it's easier to talk with someone on the phone or face to face? Why?
- Which of your friends are easier to talk with on the phone? What do they say that makes them that way?
- Who'd be the first person you'd call if you had good news…and why?
- How about if you had bad news…and why?
- How do you think you come across on the phone?
- What do you think are reasonable guidelines for your use of the telephone and for the rest of the family's use?

Chapter 13

PG May Not Mean "Pretty Good"

TELEVISION, MOVIES, VIDEOS, AND THE INTERNET

At last count my husband's video collection totaled somewhere near 546 videos. Just a second, I forgot about the stash in the drawers in his office... Back again—make that 672 videos. Oh, wait a minute. I forgot the ones standing in the corner... Back again—make that a grand total of 732. That number would not include the few dozen DVDs he's acquired, even though we do not have a DVD player yet. Or the 100+ Disney-types Bethany has in her own video cupboard.

This addiction, ironically, started more than twenty years ago when we decided not to watch television. When we built our home in our little mountain town, which literally has zilch television reception, the cable company wanted us to hand over our firstborn child as payment for underground cabling. We countered with an offer to give our Australian shepherd dog, but the cable folks said, no, dogs couldn't climb poles. We determined right then and there to do the noble, good-parenting thing. Oh, did I tell you we used to have five kids, instead of four? Just kidding... We decided to give up television forever.

Soon afterward, however, VCRs came into existence, and we succumbed. After all, we figured we could control the content of what our children watched. Instead of watching mindless sitcoms about amoral folks, we watch cowboy shoot-'em-ups, war flicks, and deadly drug dealer and detective deals, which, as everyone knows, have so much more positive influence on our youth.

While some of our videos probably wouldn't sell for a dime at a garage sale, many are worthy of watching. It was a grueling debate, but Craig and Josh agreed on the following as the Top Ten Movies of all time. You'll notice they're listed alphabetically, because they just couldn't rank them more than this.

> *Braveheart*
> *Casablanca*
> *The Godfather*
> *High Noon*
> *It Happened One Night*
> *Major Dundee*
> *Sahara*
> *Saving Private Ryan*
> *The Searchers*
> *Stagecoach*

In fact, conversations in our house often sound like those of the characters from the Top Ten list. All I did the other night was call them to dinner, and here's what transpired:

Joshua: I got a bad feeling about this one. *(sticks finger down throat)*

Bethany: When was the last time you felt good about anything?

Craig: If your mother saw you do that, she'd be very upset.

Joshua: Of all the kitchens, in all the towns, in all the world, she walks into mine.

Craig: It's like a dame; you don't feed 'em, they won't do nothing.

Bethany: I'm gonna make her an offer she can't refuse.

Joshua: That'll be the day.

Craig: There are some things a man just can't walk away from.

Bethany: Well, you gotta live, no matter what happens.

Craig: I can find another wife easy, but not a horse like this!

Joshua: That bag's worth twenty dollars!

Janet: (*approaching the trio*) You want to explain the math of this to me?

Craig: This isn't personal, Janet. This is business.

Bethany: I don't understand any of this!

Joshua: Well, I haven't got time to tell ya.

Craig: Every man dies. Not every man really lives.

Janet: "Do not forsake me, oh my darling!"

Craig: This town will be safe till tomorrow. I think I ought to stay. (*With a fork, he pulls apart a piece of the dinner's mystery meat.*)

Craig: (*saluting his wife*) Here's looking at you, kid.

Strains of "As Time Goes By" are heard as he moseys into the sunset.

What I've learned is that I should make a movie—starring ME—so my kids will take me seriously!

I'm sure the conversations in your home are also sprinkled with lines from your family's favorite movies or television shows. Sometimes those sprinklings aren't so healthy, and neither are the visual images. As accustomed as I've grown to the electronic members of our home, I'll never be accustomed to sex and violence on any screen—television, computer, or movie. We screen the films for our kids and send them out of the room for scenes we feel are inappropriate. I believe we parents need to be proactive in prayer and in practice as our kids make media choices.

Just as teens need guidance in regard to the choices they make about friendships, money, and other areas, they also need direction about media choices—all blanketed in prayer. Pornography—in movies, on television, or over the Internet—is a growing problem, even in the Christian community. One writer said that while twenty years ago 23 percent of Christians were then subscribing to pornography television channels,[25] 62 percent of *pastors and lay leaders* admitted in a magazine survey in 2000 that they regularly visit pornography sites.[26] Michael Craven, director of the Center for Decency in Dallas, Texas, told me recently that the research his organization has done indicates that these addictions are overwhelmingly born in adolescence.[27]

We need to tell our teens specifically what our guidelines are about Internet use and then pray that our children will seek purity in their private hours. Addiction to pornography leads to the destruction of marriage, families, and personal lives and even to suicide. Speak aloud against the spirit of pornography in your home and as you prayerwalk in your community. Jesus told us that the eyes are "windows into your body" (Matthew 6:22, MSG). The images we allow our eyes to view will affect our emotional and spiritual development. Even though the world is commonly viewing junk, we should pray that our children are not conforming "any longer to the pattern of this world," but instead seeking transformation by seeking after that which is good in God's sight (Romans 12:2).

Teenagers may also just want to tag along with the crowd at movie theaters—watching too much flesh on an even bigger screen. Ask ahead of time what your teen will be viewing and help your child decide what to see and what to say when the others want to watch something else. Pray that your child has the moral strength and courage to hold on to the good and to avoid the rest (1 Thessalonians 5:21-22). Films can provide a good forum for family discussion; after you watch a movie together—whether at home or in the theater—talk about the messages and values behind the movie. Ask your teen if it reflected God's fingerprints—or not—and pray for and listen to your child as you do this together.

While some teens will not be drawn to these negative media images, they may have addictions to the machines—simply watching too much television or too many DVDs or playing too much Nintendo. We can pray that our children will have self-discipline and courage to walk away from fruitless media activities (Ephesians 5:11), and we can help limit the time they spend in these activities. Instead, teens can do homework, help around the home, invite friends over to listen to music and talk, pursue a sport, take music lessons, try a new hobby, or go to youth group activities. We can turn off the television, VCR, video game, and computer and read together as a family.

Craig and I have had to limit our children's computer game time. They'd stare at a screen of any kind all day long if we let them. He loves having our kids with him and takes them out to the farm to help him; they also go to and from school with me every day. We work hard at being involved with our kids and at developing relationships with them, so we know what they're doing.

Shy kids often flee to the safety of a screen that doesn't ask embarrassing questions or require anything more than a warm body. If your kid is shy, pray that he or she will open up, and then nudge that child to get involved. Then there's the phlegmatic teen; this personality type is slow to make a decision and needs a nudge to do anything. Pray with this child over a list of some of the previous activities, and get him or her into a new routine away from the screens at home.

As we pray for our kids, we can also help them understand the importance of leading productive lives and using free time for constructive pursuits. We can make decisions to live apart from the world's influence so as to influence the world. The danger is that we view with tolerance those tasteless scenes on our televisions, at the movies, on computer games, or on the Internet. This is not a place for tolerance, as "who can bring what is pure from the impure? No one!" (Job 14:4). We can pray that our teens make choices according to the Philippians 4:8 test:

- Is it true?
- Is it noble?
- Is it right?
- Is it pure?
- Is it lovely?
- Is it admirable?
- Is it excellent?
- Is it praiseworthy?

Pray that your teen learns how to evaluate the media with these characteristics in mind so that the peace of God will be with your child as he or she chooses what to view.

I join you in your prayers for purity in your home.

Prayer for Appropriate Media Viewing

Ezekiel 20:7; Galatians 5:22-23; Ephesians 5:3,11,15-16

Lord, I sense a serious battle for my child's devotion. The Enemy is freely using media sources—television, movies, video games, and the Internet—to develop the sin of lust in good families. Help my child not to be drawn to vile images and amoral choices. I ask you to help my teen develop godly characteristics—love, joy, peace, patience, kindness, goodness, faithfulness, gentleness, and self-control. I pray that my child will live apart from the world's negative influences and will desire to follow your will. May my child see every shameful or wrong image as improper. And even if there is just a hint of immorality that could be glossed over in the name of fun, I pray my child will have nothing to do with it—always seeking light over darkness. Guide my child to use time constructively and to serve you. In Jesus' name, amen.

Teens Talk

"Bad movies do not affect me in a bad way."—Ephraim, age sixteen

"When [my parents] hear or see something inappropriate, like language, I wish they would understand that it's nothing new to me. For some reason, I guess they think they are protecting me."—Zak, age sixteen

 God Talks

1. Read Ezekiel 20.
2. What kinds of practices were the people doing that upset the Lord?
3. What do you feel was the inner, root problem of the people—the reason for their rebellion?
4. What influence did idols—vile images—have in the people's sin?
5. How do today's television, movie, and Internet images resemble the vile images spoken of in Ezekiel?

 Others Talk

It's a good idea to keep your computer and television in highly trafficked areas in your home so you can monitor what your kids are watching. Additionally, Digital Parenting columnists Elizabeth Kemper and Mark Ivey suggest that parents get serious about media controls:

- Set time limits, such as one hour per evening between seven and nine.
- Surf or play a game together.
- Review the games your child plays, and weed out the goriest ones.
- Review the dangers of chatting online with strangers.
- Set clear rules as to what kind of sites your kids can visit.

- If your child violates your guidelines, consider taking away computer privileges for a week.
- Share a screen name with your kids so you know what they're doing. Do not give your kids their own personal accounts.
- Never let your kids sign on with your screen name and password.
- Set e-mail controls to block all e-mail or just receive e-mail from known addressees.
- Consider an online timer.[28]
- Several writer friends have recommended the following for online filter services:

    Family Connect, www.familyconnect.com/start/
    N2H2, www.n2h2.com/
    Integrity On Line, www.integrity.com
    Cybersitter, www.cybersitter.com
    www.parentingteens.com/online2.shtml
    www.family.org/cforum/fnif/news/a0020749.html

You can also check out the book by Carmen Leal, *WriterSpeaker.com,* which has a section on filters and filtered Internet service providers (ISPs). Buyer beware though: The filter service I procured wouldn't let me open my own Web site even though there was nothing wrong with it! Ask questions before you commit to one. Your server should be able to help you utilize the spam filter feature on your computer so you don't get junk e-mail.

You may also want to visit the following Focus on the Family Web site for reviews of movies, CDs, and prime-time television shows: www.pluggedinmag.com. Also, TV Guardian offers a mechanical device that filters out profanity; call 1-800-967-7884.

You Talk

- What are your all-time favorite movies?
- What are your favorite television shows?

- What kind of sexual or other content makes you uncomfortable in a film?
- What guidelines do you think I should set up about the television programs or movies you watch—at home or elsewhere?
- What kinds of guidelines do you think are appropriate for using the computer, especially the Internet and e-mail?

Chapter 14

Why I Have No Life, Part 1

SPORTS AND ACTIVITIES

I've decided that sports have a lot to do with driving. Of course, I'm *driving* my kids all the time to their events. The coaches look for *drive* in kids to help the team succeed. And they ARE *driving*...they're driving me crazy!

Just this week I was driving again...not my car—a golf cart! I was the scorekeeper for a threesome of young men in Joshua's golf tournament. However, this, I decided, was fun. It wasn't like basketball scorekeeping, where I couldn't blink for fear of missing the next three-pointer or foul. It wasn't like baseball scorekeeping, where I had to learn a different language—the gestures and grunts of the ump—and keep track of who did what where. I got to relax a little, watch the geese go by, and observe the subtleties that go on between teenage boys who don't know one another.

Golf is a gentleman's sport. While there are certainly exceptions on the pro circuits—and also with Joe Duffers—those who play learn to follow the rules and etiquette. Unlike basketball, where you raise a ruckus when the opposing team's players shoot a free throw, in golf every player hushes for a drive, chip, or putt, no matter who's doing it. Unlike football, where the fans yippee when the other team's kicker misses the extra point, in golf my boys cheer when another player's ball drops into the hole. They help each other find their balls, stay out of the line of sight while another makes an approach shot, and hold the flag straight to help someone else align a putt. When one of the boys DQ'd (disqualified) over a technical issue, the others encouraged him to play the final couple of holes with them anyway.

My faith in the next generation was restored in four hours' time with eighteen holes of golf. And while someone might question the sanity of chasing a ball around until it falls into a hole, here are some life lessons my sons and I have decided grow out of the game of golf.

Life Lesson One: Pick up After Yourself. For twenty-four mothering years I have been trying to get my kids to pick up after themselves and fix the messes they create. Their underwear, sports equipment, schoolwork, and valuable personal possessions decorate the floor of their rooms. Craig and I have spent hundreds—maybe thousands—of dollars on furniture, plastic box organizers, and storage boxes to help our kids keep their things in order. They stand empty; the floor stands full.

Instead, I should have bought our kids golf clubs as toddlers and taught them the game. Golfers fix their divots, smooth out the sand traps, and pick up their clubs and balls before going home. When my son needs new carpeting, I'm going to put in Astroturf instead—maybe he'll keep it as spotless as the greens he leaves.

Life Lesson Two: Be Nice. My father, Bob Holm, always said there should just be one law in life: Be nice. That pretty much covers it all, right? Instead of cutting someone off in traffic, let the other guy go ahead. Instead of cheating on your taxes, give Uncle Sam a little extra. Instead of copying your friend's CD, go out and buy the thing.

I've already shown you how polite young golfers can be. This was also demonstrated at the first tee, which stood on a hill overlooking five hundred yards of trees, water, and sand. Here was the conversation:

Golfer 1: Why don't you go first?

Golfer 2: Oh, that's okay. Why don't YOU go first?

Golfer 3: That's all right. Why don't YOU go first?

Golfer 4: Oh, I couldn't. Why don't YOU go first?

And so on. I finally put the names in alphabetical order on the card, and they whacked away…and away…and away.

Life Lesson Three: Accept Your Penalties. When my kids got in trouble, they always whined when we sent them to their rooms, gave them extra chores, or removed a privilege. We should have sent them to golf camp when they were two years old. In golf if you use the wrong ball or hit it somewhere you're not supposed to or make some other mistake, you get one or two penalty strokes. One of the young men in our group hit his ball into the creek. He politely reported this to me and took his penalty stroke when he removed the ball. No complaints, no cusses, no angry smirks, no golf clubs thrown to the clubhouse.

Instead he said, "I won't do that again."

Parents: Raise golfers, not kids!

Life Lesson Four: Try, Try Again. At the end of the tournament I was anxious to find out how Joshua had fared. Let's just say it wasn't his best game. He'd lost three balls—and that was the first hole! The sand was magnetized to his balls, he was sure, and he whiffed one on the seventeenth hole ("whiffing" means you swung and missed—sort of a strike one in golf, because it counts for a point).

"So," I said, "you're ready to quit?"

"Quit?" he said. "No, can we stop at the driving range on the way home?"

Wouldn't it be great if all our kids' pursuits matched the passion of the average golfer, even Joe Duffer? I love that never-give-up mentality, even if it costs me another bucket of balls. Think of it: Instead of accepting the low SAT score, Johnny says, "Gee, Mom, can I take it again?" And then STUDIES this time!

As parents all we want for our kids is to be happy, right? Somehow, we construe "happy" to mean sports teams and lessons and clubs and offices and pets and a host of other things that keep all of us wondering how we're all going to make it through a week when our full calendar overlaps with life necessities, such as eating, sleeping, and breathing.

As we're considering priorities for our kids' and our own schedules, we can trust that our Father knows best. As part of the prayer process, we can consider several questions. What does the child really want? What do we want for our child? Can we agree on what's best? Pray for a partnership with your teen in regard to sports or lessons or other activities, because your child needs your positive support. "Do two walk together unless they have agreed to do so?" (Amos 3:3). I've seen kids with no parental support at games, and I've seen other kids whose parents are pushing them to perform at piano and voice recitals when they'd rather be riding a horse.

On the other hand, sometimes we parents can see potential in our children that they do not. Sometimes they need a little push. For example, did you start piano lessons as a child, convince your parents to let you quit, and now wish that you'd continued? We know from James 1:5 that we can ask God for wisdom as we're helping our kids develop their gifts and he will give it generously to us.

As our kids compete and perform, we can also pray that we'll trust God for their successes and also for their safety. Because God gifted our teenagers with their various athletic and creative abilities, we can trust him for our kids' results. We know that

> It is God who arms me with strength
>> and makes my way perfect.
> He makes my feet like the feet of a deer;
>> he enables me to stand on the heights.
> He trains my hands for battle;
>> my arms can bend a bow of bronze.
> You give me your shield of victory;
>> you stoop down to make me great.
> You broaden the path beneath me,
>> so that my ankles do not turn. (2 Samuel 22:33-37)

Recognizing that God is the provider of ability can take pressure off. He will make it all happen!

Lastly, we'll also want to pray that our teen will have the right priorities. Performance-oriented activities can put the kid front and center, developing a more-than-healthy ego and self-orientation. It's also possible that all the extracurricular fun can eat into our teen's main job—schoolwork. While as a teacher I know that opportunities abound for teens who work hard in school, as a parent I also know that all of my child's talents aren't met in the classroom. Some kids will find their life's niche in motocross or horse shows or snowboarding. (We have a young man at our school who competes at the international level half of his school year.) When we're blessed with such a child, we can pray that he or she will "throw off everything that hinders and the sin that so easily entangles," running his race "with perseverance" and fixing his "eyes on Jesus, the author and perfecter of our faith" (Hebrews 12:1-2). When our child is doing it all for Christ, keeping the right priorities and right balance, the results are up to God—in both the classroom and the activity.

Prayer for Sports and Activities
2 Samuel 22:33; Hebrews 12:1; James 1:5; Psalm 24:7,5

Father, thank you for gifting my child with his own special abilities—whether in sports or music or other activities. When my child succeeds, help him to remember that *you* are the one who arms him with his strengths, that *you* make his way perfect, that *you* enable him to succeed. When my teen is struggling, help him to run with perseverance the race marked out for him. Give me your wisdom, Lord, as I guide this child to pursue his passions and giftedness. If my teen and I get too wrapped up in the competition and the winning, remind us both not to trust in these pursuits of the world but to trust in your name. May we both shout for joy in your name when my child does well and even when things don't go his way. In Jesus' name, amen.

Teens Talk

"I must do something else other than go home. I must have a life."—Jessica, age sixteen

"It's okay for my parents to limit my activities, but I need a good reason and cooperation. I want to be encouraged in something."—Alana, age seventeen

God Talks

1. Read 2 Samuel 22:33-37.
2. According to this passage, how does God actively participate in our lives?
3. How could we help him in that activity?
4. Read Psalm 20:4-8.
5. What should our attitudes and expectations be as we trust God for our children and their activities?

Others Talk

If your family has a sports fanatic kid and you're frazzled, you might want to invest in a magazine, *Sports Parents*. The following was gleaned from two articles from the magazine's online source, www.sikids.com *(Sports Illustrated for Kids/Sports Parents)*.

- Write their schedules on a calendar.
- Take your work with you to get something done as you sit at their practices.

- Forgive yourself if you need to miss a game or two or get family and friends to sub for you.
- Set limits that fit your family.
- Resist the urge to coach your kid to and from games.
- Take advantage of driving time to talk with your kids.
- Cheer for other people's kids.
- Pack healthy food and water.
- Protect your child with quality equipment.
- Organize a spot in your child's room for the sports equipment that has to be quickly grabbed.
- Give your teen a stain stick, and train him or her to pretreat his or her uniform before throwing it into the laundry.
- Set a firm schedule for homework studies.
- Call coaches in advance about doctor appointments or religious or other commitments.
- Find out the coach's expectations at the beginning of the season.
- Watch for signs of burnout—falling grades, diminishing interest, fatigue.
- Help your child set realistic priorities.[29]

You Talk

- What are your favorite sports, lessons, or other activities?
- At what sport or activity do you wish you could be the best?
- Do you think you're too busy or not busy enough?
- What would you like to do more of? What would you like to do less of?
- How can I support you in these matters?

Chapter 15

Why I Have No Life, Part 2

PEER PRESSURE AND PARTIES

The following fable has been changed only slightly to protect…certain people who may or may not exist.

Once upon a time there were Mommy Rabbit and Daddy Rabbit who had a lovely daughter rabbit named Amanda. They all lived together rather happily in a fresh patch of cabbage. Happily, that is…until Amanda turned eighteen right before she graduated from Bunny High School.

One day during the last week before graduation, Amanda came home from school and announced that she was going camping next weekend. "It's an end-of-the-year celebration," she said, "just for Bunny High graduating seniors."

"Will there be a mommy or daddy rabbit there?" Mommy Rabbit asked.

"No," said Amanda. "That would ruin everything. We need to be all by ourselves to have a good time."

The mommy rabbit thought for a moment. "So all those other parties you had while you were growing up were no fun, because there was a mommy or daddy rabbit with you? And when Daddy Rabbit took you camping with your girlfriend bunnies on your sixteenth birthday, you didn't have any fun, because he was there too?"

"Well, uh, those were fine when we were little. Now we're eighteen. We're adult rabbits, and we should be able to do whatever we want," said Amanda.

Mommy Rabbit stared at her darling daughter, who certainly looked big enough to be an adult rabbit. However, Mommybuns knew that if Amanda were REALLY an adult rabbit, she'd be living in her own cabbage patch, but she decided to save that argument for another time.

"And will there be any sauerkraut at this camping trip?" Mommy Rabbit asked.

You see, Mommy Rabbit was one savvy momma. Because she taught mathematics at Bunny High, she knew that Amanda had been hanging around Arnold a lot lately. Arnold, who was a popular rabbit, was known to eat sauerkraut—until he was so punch flatulent that he couldn't stand up. Sometimes he even dried the stuff and smoked it! In fact, his parents often provided the kegs of sauerkraut for his parties. Mommy Rabbit had heard Arnold's father once say he'd rather have them chug the stuff at home rather than on a lonely road somewhere.

But Mommy and Daddy Rabbit didn't want Amanda eating sauerkraut at all! After all, that was a Cabbage Patch Rule.

"Um, no, Mommy, I don't think there'll be any sauerkraut there. We just want to have a good time. It's the very last time we'll all be together—the whole rabbit graduating class. It's a bonding thing, Ma!" Amanda's nose began to twitch.

"I'm sorry, Amanda," said Mommy Rabbit. "You know what your father and I have always said. There must be a parent present at a party—even if it's a camping trip—and you may not go if there's even a sniff of a possibility of sauerkraut. The only way you could go is if your father went also."

"You just don't trust me! You just don't trust me!" Amanda screamed as she punched one cabbage head after another, up and down the rows in the otherwise-peaceful garden.

When Amanda finally quieted down to a whimper, Mommybuns, who was one wise teacher, said, "I do trust you. However, I also believe this somewhat mathematical equation: You + friends + sauerkraut = probable mistakes."

So Amanda did not go on the camping trip, where there was not just one keg of sauerkraut but two. Amanda and her closest friends, who also weren't allowed to go, had their own party at home—with their parents present—and she somewhat sulkily admitted that she had a good time anyway.

Some years later, after Amanda had finished college and was teaching her own students mathematics, she one day e-mailed Mommy Rabbit.

> Dear Mother,
>
> I don't know what to do. Little Mandie wants to go camping with her friends. I'm sure there's going to be sauerkraut there, Mommybuns. What do I tell her?
>
> Love,
> Amanda

Again, Mommy Rabbit hit the cabbage on the head.

> Dear Amanda,
>
> Just say no.
>
> Love,
> Your daughter's grandmother

Because of the tremendous pressure on teens to conform, we parents will want to pray that our children will not "follow the crowd in doing wrong" (Exodus 23:2). Believe me, the quickest way for kids to become accepted by the popular crowd is to drink and abuse other substances at parties. In doing so, they instantly affirm each other's lifestyles. A bond—albeit negative—develops when teens drink, smoke, abuse dope, and do other illegal actions together. They share a secret life, one that separates them from parents and other authorities, and it's difficult to change that course. It's important for us to pray that our teens never start that lifestyle and to do everything we can to keep them safe and accountable.

The writer of 2 Kings says that when the people began rejecting the laws, which were put there for their own protection, "They followed worthless idols and themselves became worthless. They imitated the nations around them" (2 Kings 17:15). Ask God to keep your children from following wrong influences and to make them strong enough in their faith that they don't feel the need to imitate "the nations" of teens around them. I pray that my kids will seek to become conformed to the likeness of Christ (Romans 8:29), not to the likeness of those who would bring them down.

For that to happen, our kids will need great wisdom and discernment between right and wrong. A teen's judgment can be impaired when the situation is seen through the vision of their friends' rose-colored glasses rather than the truth of God's Word. You can pray through the wisdom proverbs, Proverbs 1–9, asking God that your teen will accept wisdom from you, actually seek it out, value it, and apply it in the throes of pressure from peers (Proverbs 2:1-6). We can't just assume that our kids know what's right. Just as the Israelites had to be taught to distinguish between the unclean and the clean (Leviticus 10:10), we will need God's help so that we can teach our children what's right and wrong and why we see things that way. When we do this, we will be equipping our children to be able to winnow out all evil (Proverbs 20:8).

Prayer for Discernment About Peer Pressure and Parties
Exodus 23:2; Romans 1:4; 8:29; Proverbs 2:1-6; 2 Kings 17:15

Lord, I ask that my child will not conform to the party crowd in doing wrong but instead will recognize the greater acceptance of being chosen by God. Please instill a deep desire to be conformed to the likeness of your Son, and may that desire impact my child's daily choices. Lord, my child will need your great wisdom and discernment to tell right from wrong. Increase that desire for wisdom as it's related in your Word. Help my teen to accept and store up those words from Scripture and to apply them when under pressure from friends. Give my child the courage and strength not to imitate other teens but instead to prove the worth you have given. In Jesus' name, amen.

 Teens Talk

"If [my mom doesn't] want me to go to a party, it makes me want to go three times as bad. Let me make my mistakes on my own."—Ephraim, age sixteen

"Trust me. I will only go with people I trust, and…I am careful about friends."—Fallon, age seventeen

 God Talks

1. Read Romans 13:12-14. In verse 14 we're told to clothe ourselves with the Lord Jesus Christ so as to avoid the kind of indecent behavior found at some parties. How do we "clothe ourselves with the Lord Jesus Christ"?

2. Read 2 Kings 17:13-15. How did the people get to the point where they had become "worthless"?

3. How do our teens think they get wisdom?

4. How could they gain it, according to Proverbs 2:1-6?

 ## Others Talk

Party Hearty: Instead of allowing your teen's friends to create your child's memories, you can celebrate the milestones in his life with the help of *Spiritual Milestones: A Guide to Celebrating Your Children's Spiritual Passages* by Jim and Janet Weidmann and J. Otis and Gail Ledbetter. It includes suggested ways to celebrate adolescence, a commitment to purity, steps toward adulthood, and graduation.

Prom Time: If your teen wants to join a postprom party at a hotel room, Sacramento deputy police chief Matt Powers has a few words of advice: "It's stupid! What do you THINK is going to occur in that hotel room? Why do you THINK they don't want any adult supervision? This is nothing new. It's been going on for years. And it creates tremendous problems for communities and for law enforcement."

He was responding to the tragic death of a Sacramento teen who was knifed when a prom party went wrong. Rick Jennings, school board president of Sacramento City Unified School District, said, "Parents might think they're being a friend to their child by condoning such parties. But everything is wrong with those situations. What's wrong with having a supervised party at home? Why don't they *want* that party at home? You have to ask yourself that."[30]

 ## You Talk

• How do you think parties differ today from when I was your age?

• Why do you think teens drink at parties?

- If you were invited to a party where you knew teens would have alcohol or drugs, would you want to go? Why or why not?
- What information do you think I should know before I approve your going to a party?
- What should be the guidelines here at home for hosting a party?

Chapter 16

Candy Is Not a Major Food Group

Eating Habits and Disorders

When I was a teenager, I believed in a balanced diet. My friends and I would take our Taco Bell tacos to McDonald's, where we added fries. With our 7-Eleven Slurpees, we had a "balanced meal." Since then I've done a lot of study on what teens eat and have discovered they have their own pyramid of food groups:

SODA

BURRITOS

HAMBURGERS

CANDY PIZZA CHIPS

I recently had a teenager explain to me that this kind of diet is balanced, because all the necessary dietary components are there. She said that since chips are made from potatoes and since pizza sauce comes from tomatoes, she was getting her three to four portions of vegetables daily.

Fruits, she found out in biology, are digested as simple carbohydrates. "And candy and soda are simple carbs too!" She promised that she drank at least two portions of soda per day and topped off most meals with Skittles, so she was getting all the fruit she needed.

"How about protein and complex carbs?" I queried, grabbing a slice of vegetable with pepperoni myself in the cafeteria line.

"No problem," she said, "if you eat a daily portion of hamburgers and burritos. Plus there's a bonus of both protein and bread with the slice of vegetable on your plate right now!"

Because this student was on a health kick that week, she headed back to the salad bar, where she loaded her Styrofoam tray with iceberg lettuce salad. I asked her why she passed up the ranch dressing.

"I'm watching my fats," she explained. "Prom's next week."

While we can joke about what teens do or do not eat, food and related eating disorders are critical concerns as we raise our kids. As I write this, I am praying for a friend's daughter and another friend's son—the latter, anorexic; the former, borderline, because she's not yet underweight. What they eat is an hour-by-hour, life-important issue. Food became the only thing the young woman felt she could control in her life after her family life fell apart. I can't detail the situation specifically, but she has felt abandoned by almost everyone but her immediate family—friends and church family included. Not eating is her way to regain some sense of power.

There are three kinds of eating disorders:

- *anorexia nervosa,* the intentional decision to starve one's self
- *binge eating disorder,* characterized by frequent episodes of uncontrolled overeating
- *bulimia nervosa,* a secret cycle of binging and purging

Ten percent of females between the ages of sixteen and twenty-five exhibit some anorexic behavior, with 1 to 2 percent suffering from anorexia nervosa.[31] Bulimia figures are similar,[32] with binge eating figures estimated much higher.[33] These women are often of normal weight and size, but their behaviors are identifiable. Red flags should go up when you observe any of the following, particularly in concert:

Binge eating:
- eating large amounts of food frequently—often in secret
- feelings of shame about eating

Bulimia:
- disappearance of food
- purging behaviors (vomit or diarrhea smells, wrappers of laxatives or diuretics)
- excessive exercise
- swelling of cheeks or jaw area
- calluses on hands and knuckles or discoloration of teeth
- odd schedule or ritual changes to accommodate purge sessions
- withdrawal from friends
- obsession with weight loss, dieting, and food

Anorexia:
- dramatic weight loss
- obsession with weight, food, and dieting
- refusal to eat certain foods
- denial of hunger
- new food rituals
- frequent excuses to avoid mealtimes
- excessive exercise
- withdrawal from friends[34]

These symptoms lead us to prayer. I once suffered from bulimia myself. I had joined a weight-loss group, because I wanted to be thin for a high school reunion some years after our third child. As I approached the scale, I made a comment to the group's leader about not doing very well on my diet that week.

I'll never forget what she said, as it started a cycle that could have proved deadly for me: "Oh, just take a laxative the night before you weigh in. That's what I do!"

Although she laughed, I took her advice seriously and started taking laxatives. At first I just took one a week, as she had advised. Soon, however, I wanted to encourage greater weight loss and began taking them nearly daily. I reached my weight goal—I even got a regional award at a convention—but I was sick all the time.

One morning I looked into the mirror and thought I saw a dead person behind my eyes. I threw away the laxative package and haven't used one since. I was fortunate that my bulimic activities only lasted a couple of months. Others find the behavior addictive, especially when it brings the desired weight loss.

If you fear your teen may be struggling with an eating disorder, pray for his or her self-perception. Television, movies, magazines, and music videos all perpetuate the myth that thin is good, thinner is better, and thinnest is best, even though some of those images may be digitally doctored. I'm letting God speak to me, too, reader friend, in this regard.

> But who are you, O man, to talk back to God? "Shall what is formed say to him who formed it, 'Why did you make me like this?'" Does not the potter have the right to make out of the same lump of clay some pottery for noble purposes and some for common use?…
>
> What if he did this to make the riches of his glory known to the objects of his mercy, whom he prepared in advance for glory? (Romans 9:20-21,23)

Why was my child or I made in such a way? As each pottery vessel has a purpose, so does each of us, in just the vessel we've been given. Finding and serving that purpose will be simpler once we decide to accept the vessel God has given us—first moms, then sons and daughters. *Young and Modern* magazine reports that in households where moms talk about feeling fat, 81 percent of their teenager girls said they felt fat too.[35] Because girls who suffer from eating disorders often have mothers who obsess about their own weight, this is where we start with prayer: that God will help us—mothers and daughters—love ourselves as he has created us ("Love your neighbor *as yourself*," Mark 12:31, emphasis added). Please note: We are not to blame for our daughters' poor choices, but we are certainly responsible for helping them learn how to make better ones.

About 10 percent of those with eating disorders who see mental health professionals are male, and they have these problems for the same reason most women do—they are not happy with their body image.[36]

The issue of power or control is also an important focus for prayer. As girls and boys head into and through puberty, they can feel powerless as their bodies change. Particularly, since girls mature more quickly than boys their age, their peers may make fun of their new shape. Discuss these issues with your teens, assure them that the changes are part of God's design for them, and pray for them and with them, helping them give over control of their body to the Lord, for "a man is a slave to whatever has mastered him" (2 Peter 2:19). We don't want to be a slave to food urges or society's values or others' opinions of us; we want to serve God with our hearts, minds, and bodies.

Next, we can pray that our children and we eat for the right reasons and recognize God's gift of hunger. We don't need food when we're depressed, tired, tense, stressed, or lonely. We need food when we're hungry, not when we need comfort. Hunger pains don't mean we're starving. They simply mean that we need refueling. Your car "dings" when you're getting low on fuel. Hunger pains do the same thing—give a little notice that a meal is in order. A scriptural prayer is that we remember that "man does not live on bread alone but on every word that comes from the mouth of the LORD" (Deuteronomy 8:3). Pray that your children will seek God, not food, for their emotional needs.

Prayer for Right Eating
Isaiah 44:24; Psalm 18:30; 1 Corinthians 6:19;
2 Peter 2:19; 2 Corinthians 12:9

Lord, who formed my child in the womb, help her to understand that you have made all things beautiful, especially her. Remind her that your way is perfect, and therefore the way you have fashioned her is perfect. Help her to recognize her body as a temple of your Spirit so she should seek out healthful eating and exercise practices that will nurture and protect your creation and therefore bring you glory. I know, Lord, that I am a slave to whatever masters me, so lead us both to healthy ways to soothe ourselves when we are depressed, stressed, tense, tired, or lonely. Help us both to have victory in this area, Lord, but if eating healthfully does prove to be a struggle, remind us that your grace is sufficient for us, for your power is made perfect in our weakness. In Jesus' name, amen.

 ### Teens Talk

"My parents should understand that I want to eat practically fat-free so I won't be overweight."—Bekau, age fourteen

"I wish my parents would understand that I like what I like."—Michael, age fourteen

 ### God Talks

1. Reflect on Romans 9:20-23.
2. Why do we question God about his design of us?
3. How do you feel about the way you look?

4. How does your self-perception affect your teen's?

5. If that's not particularly positive, how will you change your behavior in regard to how you perceive yourself?

 Others Talk

Sharon Hersh offers innumerable helps for parents in *"Mom, I Feel Fat!"* and the following directives can be followed if an eating disorder is suspected:

- Ask a youth pastor or school counselor to recommend a professional counselor.
- Contact your insurance company for information about coverage.
- Choose a therapist who focuses on adolescents and eating disorders.
- Contact the National Eating Disorder Association (918-481-4044) for a list of therapists and treatment centers in your area.
- Interview at least three therapists with your teen—and let your teen choose.
- Request that you be a part of the recovery process.
- Ask for a sliding fee scale if money is an issue.
- Ask your church about financial support for counseling. If money is not available, contact the National Mental Health Association (800-969-NMHA) for free resources in your area.[37]

Additionally, a great Web site is provided by the National Eating Disorders Association at www.nationaleatingdisorders.org. The mailing address is P.O. Box 7, Highland Park, IL 60035.

 You Talk

- What food hang-ups do you think I have?
- What dumb things have you heard me say about food, eating, or dieting?
- Do you see food as an enemy or a friend? Why?

- What would you like to know about healthy eating?
- What kind of exercise would you like to do regularly, and how can I support you in that effort?
- How do you otherwise need help in managing your eating?

Chapter 17

"Stop Saying Your Sibling's an Alien"

FAMILY RELATIONSHIPS

Before we begin this chapter, I need for you to complete the following survey:

OFFICIAL PARENTING SURVEY

Directions: Choose the answer you think is best, and write the corresponding letter on the appropriate line.

_____ 1. Siblings are not

(a) punching bags

(b) personal maids

(c) lending institutions

(d) all of the above

_____ 2. Siblings are

(a) always patient with one another

(b) always kind to one another

(c) never envious, boastful, self-seeking…you know the rest

(d) none of the above

Okay, I think we're on the same page now. My personal qualifications are too lengthy to list in regard to sibling relationships, but I'll do a modified résumé for you:

Janet M. Holm
a.k.a., "BIG SISTER" and "THE BOSS"

OBJECTIVES: To make my two brothers and two sisters absolutely miserable and to convince them I am the one in charge

EDUCATION: Graduate, Home of Hard Knocks

EXPERIENCE: *Top-Notch Teaser:* Personally teased my brother Peter so much that he became an accomplished chair and knife thrower (until I moved from home).

Savvy Snitch: Adeptly placed blame for any household messes on my younger siblings, Roberta and Matt.

Practiced Pilferer: Borrowed my sister Nancy's clothes so often that she forgot they were hers.

REFERENCES: Available upon request from any of my siblings, who are more than happy to provide them.

My husband has his own impressive résumé, with SIX siblings as credible references. So it proved to be no surprise to my parents when the four children born to Craig and me were, frankly, completely obnoxious to one another on a regular basis. For the record, I think we have one broken mirror, one smashed window, two cracked lamps, two doors that don't hang on their hinges, and seventeen chipped and/or demolished figurines. It's my opinion that stores should NOT sell figurines to people who have children under the age of thirty. Or they should just give them away prebroken and patched. Then moms wouldn't be so upset if a porcelain pigeon lost its wing to Big Time Wrestlers, because it was already mended with Super glue anyway.

I love it when I just sort of "discover" these joys of motherhood. You know what I mean. You're dusting at one minute to six, the Hour of Company, when you find out at least three things (there are probably others—you just haven't discovered them yet):

1. The marble doves, the ones you got for a wedding present from your college roommate, have been decapitated. You may have guessed that I collect bird figurines. Actually, I USED to collect them. They're all dead now except the ones made of wood. I think all figurines should be made of wood. But maybe that fact would just challenge the siblings to find even more creative ways to leave behind signs of their wrestling matches.

2. The blue-and-white ceramic lamp doesn't turn on but instead falls into three pieces.

3. And the rocking chair doesn't rock anymore. It tips your poor company to the carpeting instead. Well, maybe the plant that poor Emma rolled into wasn't so great anyway.

These are just some of the results of McHenry Sibling Insanity. Some of that results from their McHenry Competitive Gene, for which I am partly responsible. We play games, literally. We must own a hundred board games. Formerly I had to use a shoehorn to close the front hall closet door. I think the board games began to birth offspring of their own, like Win, Lose, or Trouble...or Crackers in My Pursuit...or Candy Words. To house our growing collection, I had to buy an antique cupboard so big it could bury three lumberjacks and their chain saws.

A chain saw probably couldn't be heard over the racket my kids make when they play games. That's because there are the regular rules—carefully delineated in carefully printed brochures, which are carelessly thrown out by the McHenry siblings and their father—and the McHenry rules, which vary from game to game, or more likely, from moment to moment.

The McHenry girls tend toward the word games, such as Balderdash, while the McHenry guys lean toward the war games—Risk, Battle Cry, Axis and Allies, Axis and Allies Pacific, Axis and Allies Europe...Axis and Allies Los Angeles, Axis and Allies Chicago, Axis and Allies Las Vegas... and so on.

In one-half of the room the girls are fighting about whether

- *piblockto* could be "an infectious hysteria affecting Eskimo women and dogs" (yup)
- *scaldabanco* means "a stirring preacher who delivers a wonderful sermon" (it does)
- *martext* is "an unaccomplished minister who stumbles through a sermon" (it is)[38]

(Please note the handy new words I've provided for your Sunday go-to-meetin' use.)

One of the McHenry women will win; one will lose. The loser will not go quietly into that good night, the game will remain scattered over the living room floor, and McHenry Mom will threaten to throw away half the games in the cupboard.

On the other side of the room the McHenry guys are blitzing Europe, blasting Asia, and bombing Greenland. (Bomb Greenland? Why? I've always wondered.) Their pleasant conversation sounds something like, "I'm gonna take Western Europe" and "Well, I'm goin' after Ontario" and "I'm hittin' ya hard here." Ouch. Then when they argue about the current McHenry rules, they come close to hittin' each other, and the game's over. Like the game on the eastern side of the battleground, the losers will not go quietly either. The game will remain scattered over the dining room table, and McHenry Mom will threaten to use a chain saw to cut the game cupboard in half and use it for firewood…even though we have no wood stove!

Arrrggghhh!

Healthy competition could be excused, but when my kids compare themselves with each other on grades, appearance, or privileges ("You let Josh go—why can't I?"), it's time for prayer. Resentment and jealousy form the worm that can eat at family relationships, as many Bible stories teach. Cain, jealous because God favored Abel's offering over his own, killed his brother (Genesis 4:2-16). Esau held a grudge against his brother, Jacob, because Jacob had stolen from their father the blessing that should have been his own, saying, "The days of mourning for my father are near; then I will kill my brother Jacob" (Genesis 27:41). Joseph's brothers plotted to kill him. "When his brothers saw that their father loved him more than any of them, they hated him and could not speak a kind word to him" (Genesis 37:4). We learn that Jacob "kept the matter in mind," which was probably a mistake; he should have given the matter to prayer (Genesis 37:11).

The story of the older brother of the prodigal son shows the ugliness of jealousy. When the prodigal returned, his older brother resented that their father welcomed home the son who had left him to do all the work (Luke 15:11-32). I find it interesting that it took longer for the older son and father to reconcile (and maybe they didn't) than it did for the younger, prodigal son and father. Perhaps the sin of jealousy has a deeper root that takes a stronger hold in our lives than the sins of greed and self-orientation.

We can pray in many specific ways that can guard against jealousy and what may seem like natural rivalry. We parents will want to pray that we'll "do nothing out of favoritism" (1 Timothy 5:21), which could "exasperate" (Ephesians 6:4) and "embitter" (Colossians 3:21) our children, so they will not become discouraged.

We can also pray that our teens will not harbor bitter envy toward any brother or sister or hold selfish ambition in their hearts (James 3:14). We can also intercede that God will deepen their love for each other and that they will become considerate, submissive, and merciful in their dealings with each other—peacemakers right in your own home (James 3:17). I pray that my kids will become one another's best friends—may yours, as well.

Prayer for Love
1 Corinthians 13; 1 Timothy 5:21; James 3:14,17

Father, I ask for your kind of love in our home, especially between our children. I pray my children will demonstrate patience with one another. Help them to be kind as well—to understand someone else may need the things of our home and to recognize when someone needs an understanding word or act of kindness. Lord, break any bond of jealousy or sense of self-importance. May my children not anger easily when things don't go their way, and may they forgive quickly when offense is made. Help me never to favor one child over another so no root of jealousy can develop. I pray that my kids will not harbor envy or selfishness in their hearts but instead demonstrate consideration and mercy toward each other that has grown out of love. It is my desire that my family will exist to protect one another, trust one another, and love when others' love fails. In Jesus' name, amen.

Teens Talk

"Just because my sister and I fight does not mean we don't love each other."—Bekau, age fourteen

"Don't get mad if I'm fighting with my sister then later laughing."—Jessica, age sixteen

God Talks

1. Read Genesis 27:41-46. How did the brothers' actions affect the family as a whole?
2. After twenty years of separation, Jacob prepared to meet his brother. Read Genesis 32:1-21. How was Jacob feeling? What did he think would happen at their meeting?
3. Read Genesis 33:1-11. Who took the first step to approach the other?
4. How do you think their reconciliation affected each of them?
5. What principles about family relationships can you draw from this story?

Others Talk

When parents divorce and remarry, the blended families face some tremendous challenges. In *Angry Kids: Understanding and Managing the Emotions That Control Them,* Richard L. Berry makes the following recommendations, many of which are also applicable for parents who have not divorced:

- Take time to grieve the losses and changes associated with the divorce.
- Be realistic in your stepfamily expectations, and make them known.
- Try to keep the children in the same school as before.
- Maintain the usual activities if possible.
- Provide substitute roles or chores when blended families establish new routines so no one feels replaced.
- Prioritize regular time alone with your biological child.
- Avoid the need to choose sides.
    —Don't ask your child to choose or like the stepparent over the biological parent.
    —Don't make your child call the stepparent "Mom" or "Dad."
    —Don't bad-mouth the other parent.
    —Don't tell your child he or she doesn't have to listen to or obey his or her other biological parent's new spouse.
- Clarify, agree upon, and apply reasonable rules, expectations, and consequences to all the children in the home.
- Initially have the biological parent make the bulk of the discipline decisions.
- Inform your children of the stepparent's authority and jurisdiction.
- Elicit and pay close attention to the child's opinions.
- Help your child distinguish between those things he or she can change and those he or she must accept.[39]

You Talk

- What bothers you most about your brother or sister?
- What qualities do you especially like in him or her?

- What do you think bugs your brother or sister about you?
- What do you think he or she appreciates the most about you?
- What could you do so that you would get along better?

Chapter 18

Late Bloomers Become Full-Flowered

DATING AND SEX

Craig's and my rule about dating was simple. We jokingly said once, "You can date when you're eighteen and out of our home."

That was when we had the mind-set that someone should not only raise the legal drinking age and driving age but also raise the legal puberty age. Science is really the problem, you know. Even our former doctor agreed. He said "too much testosterone" was the problem with the world. And even though my kids' hormones were somewhat late in kicking things into gear, they showed up with a vengeance that year, so I had to agree. Too many hormones in the air.

Fortunately, my kids haven't dated a lot in high school. As I mentioned, Craig and I discouraged that. After all, he and I met in Arnie Zimbelman's U.S. history class at Elk Grove High. The rest was history, I guess you could say.

Our first date was the junior prom. When Craig invited me, I wasn't too sure about him, as I'd never heard him speak before. He is a man of few words. But since it was my birthday, I did not want to spend the evening at home watching Carol Burnett, so I accepted his invitation.

I have a few vague memories about the evening. I remember his reaction to my bouffant hairdo: "What did you do to your hair?" He later told me that the feature of mine he liked the most was my soft, long hair—not ratted, teased, and sprayed stuff. I just don't understand why.

I remember ordering lamb chops for dinner and seeing a look of horror on his face, and then I noticed it was the most expensive thing on the menu. Oops.

I remember a very bouncy two-step that had nothing to do with the beat of any song played during the entire evening. We've since taken ballroom dancing lessons, and the instructor gave up trying to help Craig keep the beat. (Don't ask him to sing either.)

And I remember his driving. It had nothing to do with the lines in the road. I had been taught that you're generally supposed to drive inside the lines on the road—you know in a parallel-sort of fashion. He was all over the place in that brown-and-tan '57 Chevy. Later I learned he did not even have his driver's license and only got to use the car because of a deal he'd made with his mom. She had told him that he could use the car if he could fix it, thinking that wasn't very likely. Well, Craig can be one resourceful person, and Mom McHenry had to hand over the keys for the night to keep her word.

That night I learned that prayer works.

As Craig said only about a dozen words all night long, that was our only date for almost a whole year. And then the next February, in our senior year, I saw him looking at me across the floor at a high school dance, and I remember thinking, *I think that guy loves me.*

I was right. We dated for four and a half years and married after we'd both finished our undergraduate degrees. If there's one thing we agree on in regard to parenting, it's the dating game. After all, look what happened to us.

Dating, which is not specifically addressed in the Bible, is actually a twentieth-century phenomenon that grew with the development of the automobile, which made it easier to get across town for an evening. While there are valid arguments for and against dating (I offer resources on both sides), teens are probably going to have infatuations, no matter what we say, pray, or do. Some kids are so shy, they won't act on their feelings, but those who are more confident will. Because infatuation can lead to physical attraction, it's important that teens have a solid grounding in what God's Word says about the two kinds of purity he wants for his children, and our prayers can be focused in these two ways.

First, God wants us to remain sexually pure. Even though we can be forgiven of our sexual mistakes, those mistakes may haunt us for a long time. Paul wrote that since our bodies are members of Christ himself, we need to flee from sexual immorality (1 Corinthians 6:15,18). We are to honor Christ with our bodies, because each is a temple, a home, for the Holy Spirit (verses 19-20). Sex is a privilege reserved for only those who are married to each other. So as our kids mature physically, we should pray that they will save themselves completely for the one they will marry.

The second area of purity relates to faith. We serve a God who is jealous of our devotion; he does not want us bound in any way to those who serve other gods. As wise as Solomon was, he made stupid mistakes about his personal life in marrying women who served other gods, even after God had told the Jews, "You must not intermarry with them, because they will surely turn your hearts after their gods" (1 Kings 11:2). God doesn't care about the color of our skin as we choose our mate, but he does care that the spiritual color of our hearts be the same—two hearts both passionately beating after him. I've prayed since my kids were little that they would choose a mate who was sold out for God.

"How will I know?" Rebekah once asked me.

"He will be your friend first," I said, "and it will be clear that he loves God more than he loves you—and that will be what attracts you to him."

Rebekah found such a man in Ozvaldo Perez, a man whose heart is sold out for God, and they married in June 2001, a month after she graduated from college. God answered both prayers for purity with our Ozzie.

Prayer for Purity

Proverbs 2:11-12; 1 Corinthians 6:18; Colossians 3:5;
Proverbs 4:23; 1 Kings 11:2; 1 Corinthians 5:11

Lord, there's so much confusion in the Christian community about dating. Help me know what you would have me teach my teenager about sex, dating, and marriage. Please give my child discretion and understanding as he has opportunities to be with the opposite sex so that he demonstrates self-control. Help him to heed your cautionary guidance and flee from sexual immorality, making the decision to remain pure. Teach him to put to death those desires of an earthly nature, which are not of you. Guard his heart so he will be ready to commit himself in marriage only to someone who passionately loves you, Lord. Guide our home in such a way that we can openly discuss these matters of relationship, which are so crucial. In Jesus' name, amen.

 ## Teens Talk

"Sex is something best reserved for marriage. Dating is good when done right."—Brett, age eighteen

"I wish my parents knew the temptations and the urge and pressure."—Michael, age fourteen

 ## God Talks

1. Read 1 Corinthians 6:12-20.
2. Why is self-control important if God does not judge us by our behavior?

3. What kinds of consequences could occur from sexual immorality, beyond the obvious physical ones, according to the passage?
4. How do you think your teenager feels about sexual relations outside of marriage?
5. How could you advise your teen in practical terms to avoid situations that could lead to sex?

 Others Talk

In *I Kissed Dating Goodbye,* Joshua Harris recommends abandoning traditional dating patterns and pursuing a different way of developing a relationship. While the book is geared for a single reader, it provides good guidance as we teach our kids about how to build a relationship. The following is adapted from the book.

- Determine whether a relationship will be God-honoring or merely self-satisfying.
- Seek a deeper friendship first.
    —Find activities that pull you both into each other's world of family, friends, work, service, and ministry.
    —Avoid saying and doing things that express romantic love.
    —Don't flirt.
    —Don't encourage your friends to talk about you or treat you as a couple.
    —Avoid being paired off by inviting others to join you.
- Seek God in prayer about the relationship.
- Seek the counsel of a few trusted, older Christians and ask them to pray as well.
- Wait. You don't need to rush.
- Ask: Would I consider marrying this person? If not, end the relationship.

- If marriage seems possible, discuss this potentiality with the other person and his or her parents.
- Honor the parents' desires in this regard, and invite their questions.
- Test and build the relationship in real-life settings—through serving and interacting with others (not living together!).
- Reserve passion for marriage.[40] Harris quotes Elisabeth Elliot: "Keep your hands off and your clothes on."[41]

In *I Gave Dating a Chance,* Jeramy Clark writes:

- "The goals of a dating relationship should be to honor God while you get to know another person and, yes, to develop the skills eventually needed in marriage."
- "Marriage itself should not be the only target in sight as you date. You have to learn to view each dating relationship as a step in learning and growing."
- "What I am convinced of is this: *God's will is that you become the person He desires,* and not that you become obsessed with your search for The One."
- "Some things *should* be nonnegotiable on your [future spouse] list, such as a long and constant walk with Christ, a heart for the lost, and compassion. But surface traits and characteristics should never become essentials."
- "Dating itself should not become the central focus of your life. Dating should be a healthy means of personal growth for you, allowing you to develop your relationship skills and to prepare for the future in a way that honors God."[42]

To date or not to date? You and your teen might want to give both books a chance before deciding what's right. Another helpful piece of advice comes from Kevin Leman in *Adolescence Isn't Terminal.* He says teens should prepare a list of their own dating guidelines and discuss them with their parents before they go out on their first date, noting that this helps to prevent them from allowing situations to get out of control.[43]

You Talk

- Describe the kind of person you would like to marry someday.
- What do you think are the most important qualities of a husband or wife?
- What is it about good marriages that makes them work?
- How do you feel about dating?
- What do you think should be the guidelines in our family about dating?

Chapter 19

Vaulting the Golden Arches
Is Not a Life Plan

GOALS

As the staff member at our high school who teaches all of the junior and senior English classes, I often chat with my students about their postgraduation plans. I've never made my students write an essay on "What I Want to Be When I Grow Up," although I do help them with their college application essays.

Often, however, I'll have a conversation like this:

"Hey, Krista, what are your plans for next year?"

"I'm going to marry Bart, Mrs. McHenry."

I try not to make a face. "What if there is no Bart, hon?"

"But there is—we've been going together for three months, and he's the one for me."

"What if there is no Bart in three more months?"

She rolls her eyes. "Oh, but he loves me. See? He gave me this necklace for my birthday."

"What if there is no Bart for the next birthday?"

"Oh, but there will be. And he's going to buy me a horse ranch, and I'm going to train horses for a living."

"What if there is no Bart to buy a horse ranch?"

"Oh, there will be, and I'll just love training horses with Bart."

Just for the record, this was a real conversation, with the names changed, and there was no Bart on graduation day. Krista moved to the big city to train horses and found that people who can afford to pay someone to shovel their horses' manure don't think much of those little-town girls who do that for a living. A few months later she moved back with her parents, disillusioned.

In reality, disagreements about life goals can create a lot of tension at home. We parents often have a prescription of sorts for our kids—an idea of what we think will make them happy, what we think they should do. We know what's worked or not worked for us and hope to guide our kids to a path we think will relieve them of pain. The best thing we can do, however, is to encourage our teens to seek God's plan for their lives and pray for them and with them in this regard. "Many are the plans in a man's heart, but it is the LORD's purpose that prevails.... The fear of the LORD leads to life: Then one rests content, untouched by trouble" (Proverbs 19:21,23). God's purpose is that we grow closer to him and glorify him with our lives.

Most kids today desire a comfortable—even rich—life. Often they plan a college and career path that's completely focused on the acquisition of wealth. We learn from the Proverbs verse, however, that contentment comes from living within God's framework. We can pray, then, that our children will seek his plans—"plans to prosper you and not to harm you, plans to give you hope and a future" (Jeremiah 29:11). For these plans to fall into place, we should intercede that our teen will seek God with all his or her heart (Jeremiah 29:13). It's my desire, personally, that God will figuratively enlarge my children's tent—their sphere of influence as believers—and that he will use them to further his kingdom.

Some teens have no idea about what to pursue after high school. I hold conferences with each of my seniors every fall about their yearlong senior projects, which are often centered on a career that intrigues them. Every year I'll hear at least one senior tell me, "I'm not interested in anything." What that statement usually means is "I'm not interested in anything you think I should be interested in." Sometimes we parents quickly dismiss our kids' goals as not being as ambitious as we'd like. When that's the case, we can pray that we will encourage our children to live lives worthy of God (1 Thessalonians 2:11-12)—and remember that his Son worked honorably as a carpenter most of his adult life.

By the time my children graduate from high school, they will have taken at least four different career or aptitude tests—all designed to help them identify their natural abilities and vocational interests. This is certainly helpful, but I also pray that I can help my children recognize their spiritual gifts. Few aptitude tests would suggest that a young man become a pastor or exercise a gift of exhortation. We can pray over the spiritual gifts passages from Ephesians 4:11-13, 1 Corinthians 12:27-31, and Romans 12:6-8 as we ask God to speak clearly to kids about his will for their lives. We can also teach these passages to our children, help them identify their spiritual gifts, and encourage them to use them.

When each of our two older kids were high school seniors, their youth group leader, Anne, held prayer meetings in the fall with the seniors of our church and their parents. As the teens and parents sat in a circle, each parent answered the following questions:

- What is your child's greatest strength?
- Where do you see your child in five to ten years?
- What is your greatest fear for your child?

The teens then answered the following questions after hearing from their parents:

- Where do you see yourself in five to ten years?
- What is your greatest fear?
- What is the greatest thing you learned from each of your parents?
- What does God want from you right now?

We all then committed to a twenty-four-hour period of fasting and prayer that God would speak clearly to our senior teens. (Another year some of the time was dedicated to prayer, forgiveness, and reconciliation—an important issue for those particular teens and their parents.) A week later we met again to share how God had spoken—directly or through his Word—and prayed together for our kids' futures.

Those kids saw God do amazing things for them over the next six months—full scholarships to good universities, marriages to godly spouses, and protection overseas during military tours. They are now serving God in their own churches and workplaces as an accountant, a vet school student, teachers, and other admirable professions. We parents and teens together dedicated the next years to God, and he honored those commitments.

Ultimately, I hope that all my children will honor the Lord with their lives. In Jeremiah 45:4-5, God says that he will not honor our plans and will even overthrow what he has built if we do not honor him. My highest prayer, then, as my child considers her future, is that however she lives her life, she will glorify God in all possible respects.

Prayer for My Child's Future
Jeremiah 29:11-14; Proverbs 4:5; 19:20-23; 4:25-27; Isaiah 54:2

Father, I know that your plans for my child are to prosper her, not harm her, and to give her hope and a future. I pray that my child will seek you with her whole heart, pray, and then listen to your specific words for her. Lead my teen away from anything that would keep her heart captive, that is not in your will, and remind her of those times you carried her so she will develop a lifelong trust in you. I pray that my child will get wisdom and understanding from your Word and learn to set aside her own plans and seek your purpose instead. May my child look straight ahead, fixing her gaze on you and not swerving to the right or the left—knowing that you will make level paths for her feet. Enlarge the sphere of her influence, Lord, so the light you've placed within her will reach to others for your glory. In Jesus' name, amen.

 Teens Talk

"My goals are not in education; they're more spiritual and with relationships."—Jessica, sixteen

"My parents create my goals.... I want to make them."—Jason, sixteen

 God Talks

1. Read the passages on spiritual gifts: Romans 12:6-8; 1 Corinthians 12:27-31; Ephesians 4:11-13. Make a list of the gifts mentioned.
2. What gifts do you think you have? How do you use them?
3. What gifts do you think your teenager has? How does he or she use them?
4. Make another list that includes jobs that would employ those gifts. Pray over the list, asking God what his plans are.

 Others Talk

In *And Then I Had Teenagers,* Susan Alexander Yates suggests the following as a prayerful strategy for plans after high school:

- Pray that God will make the choice clear to your teen.
- Consider that the two years postgraduation are critical to your teen's faith development.

- If your teen isn't heading for college, encourage him or her to think about a year or two working for a missions organization such as Youth With A Mission (YWAM) or at a Christian conference center. Encourage your child to consider at least two similar kinds of opportunities and pray about the choice.
- For those who want to go to college:
    —Make an appointment with the school guidance counselor before the high school freshman year to plot a strategy for classes your child will need to qualify for the kinds of colleges in which he or she is interested. (I'd add: Do that yearly.)
    —Make a list of the criteria your teen considers important in choosing a college: location (city or small town), size, cost, type of academic challenge, Christian fellowship.
    —Investigate the Christian fellowship opportunities at each school.
    —Visit the schools. (I'd add: Do this before the senior year begins.) See if your teen can stay in a dorm and visit classes while they're in session.
    —Agree (teen and parents) together on approximately five colleges to apply to. Finish the applications early in the fall of the high school senior year. (I'd add: Make sure you file the separate financial aid application with each school on time—you may need to request the form in addition to the entrance application. Also file the Free Application for Federal Student Aid form between January 2 and March 2 of the senior year; go to www.fafsa.ed.gov for information. This form is how universities determine the amount of financial aid they will offer students each year.)
- Make the decision after the acceptance and rejection letters come. (I'd add: Decisions are usually due by May 1 of the senior year,

and you should wait until you receive each college's financial aid offer before deciding.)

- Plan for the adventure ahead. Good advice to give your teen: Get to know one professor well and visit that professor outside of class, adopt a family at church and spend time with them, spend time with different kinds of people, attend a fellowship meeting at least three times before deciding if it's the right one, wear a T-shirt with a Christian logo on it on moving-in day and during the first few days, which will help connect with other believers. (I'd add: Prayerfully fill out the dorm roommate survey. My advice to college freshmen consists of two rules: Do the reading before you go to class, and go to class. Craig's and my advice to parents: A freshman doesn't need a car—it's just a distraction from good study habits.)
- Pray for the details, such as a mentor, good friends, and his or her personal goals.[44]

If your teen isn't interested in college, you can encourage independence by helping your teen

- investigate trade schools that teach specific job skills,
- prepare a professional résumé,
- plan a job-hunting strategy,
- practice for job interviews,
- choose appropriate clothing for job hunting,
- check out careers with the various branches of the military,
- estimate living expenses, prepare a monthly budget, and plan a timetable for moving out.

You Talk

- What is the class you enjoy the most in school? Why do you think that's so?

- What do you think are your greatest gifts or talents?
- What would be your dream job?
- What kinds of things do you enjoy doing the most?
- What do you think God's plans are for you—in the near future and down the road?

Chapter 20

Temptations...but Not the Singing Group

Smoking, Alcohol, Drugs

Fact: Use of ecstasy, a mild hallucinogen linked to long-term neurological changes, is growing faster than use of any other drug; in 2000, 11 percent of high school seniors had used it, almost twice the 1998 rate of 5.8 percent.[45]

Fact: My idea of ecstasy in high school was learning we didn't have to do a lab report after a chemistry experiment.

Fact: Drugs are everywhere, easy to obtain, and hard to avoid.[46]

Fact: The only substances at my friends' parties were onion dip and diet soda.

Fact: Among high school seniors, 49 percent have smoked marijuana, according to a study by the University of Michigan. In fact, 6 percent smoke pot daily. By contrast, 29 percent of adults over the age of thirty-five have smoked marijuana, according to the National Household Survey on Drug Abuse.[47]

Fact: When my college roommate and I smelled grass next door, we first thought it was the alfalfa fields across the road.

Fact: Sixty-two percent of high school seniors have gotten drunk during their lives. Thirty percent of seniors—and 14 percent of eighth graders—had consumed five or more drinks in a row during the two weeks before the Michigan survey.[48]

Fact: I drank on a weekly basis as an adolescent—but only at the communion rail in our church.

Fact: The drug of choice is often alcohol.[49]

Fact: I thought parties with kegs served root beer.

Fact: Nationwide, 28.5 percent of high school students in 2001 reported they had smoked a cigarette in the previous month.[50]

Fact: The closest thing I did to smoking was stoking the high school bonfire during homecoming.

Fact: I am obviously a very old person now (that's 'cause I think wedgies and thongs are shoes), but I'm a lot wiser.

Fact: More teens than not are doing at least some of these things today. I know this not only because I'm an experienced mom, but also because I hear teenagers talk in the hallways and read their poetry and other writings—even passed notes. They tell me what they and their friends are doing.

Fact: We need to become a lot wiser as parents and more proactive as pray-ers, because these substances can kill our kids.

When my two older kids were in high school, I prayed that they wouldn't become popular. They could have been nerds. (My personal motto is, I'm proud to be a nerd.) They could have been hicks. They could have been techies. They could have been anything as far as I was concerned—but just not popular. I knew that "cigarettes," "beer," and "drugs" were the passwords to popularity, and I didn't want my kids using that vocabulary.

Imagine my horror, then, on one lunch break when I realized that Rebekah and Justin were being sought after. They were riding in cars off-campus. They were popular! Ack!

I remember thinking, *What am I going to do?*

Could I do something to make them unpopular? Could I make the senior research paper thirty pages long instead of ten? Could I assign *The Rise and Fall of the Third Reich* for weekend reading? Could I make my students memorize *Hamlet* backward?

No, I knew I couldn't do that.

Instead, I made them memorize *Hamlet* in the correct order.

No, I'm just kidding, although I did give some thought to making them memorize the "To be or not to be…" speech.

I thought it should read something like this:

> To be popular or not to be popular: that is the question:
> Whether 'tis nobler in the mind to suffer
> The slings and arrows of outrageous smirks,
> Or to take beer with a sea of jocks,
> And by drinking join them? To be ignored;
> No more; and by a joint we end
> The heartache and the thousand nightmares
> That unpopularity is heir to, 'tis a hope
> Devoutly to be wish'd…
>   …Soft you now!
> The fair jockette, in her eyes
> Be all my coolness remember'd.

The problem was, I thought they might not read between my farcical lines and recognize the false "truth" into which they were buying!

No, I couldn't have stopped how others perceived my kids, popular or not. Both Craig and I still kept watch over their comings and goings—kept the reins tight as they failed to demonstrate trustworthiness. They slipped out of those reins at times, made their mistakes, and learned from them. I prayed over our kids through that season—that God in his mercy would watch over them and keep them from harm.

A key verse I prayed was, "Do not follow the crowd in doing wrong" (Exodus 23:2). It's a terrible temptation—that lure to drink or smoke or do drugs—with the promise of popularity attached. The Enemy often deceives our kids, however. He makes them believe that they can simply play with these substances and achieve automatic acceptance. There is some truth to this. I've seen kids talking in the hall after a weekend of indulgence together; there's a bond that forms between those who have abused together. They laugh about what they've done; they rag on parents who've turned them in; and they make fun of the authorities who have written them up.

We parents will want to pray that our kids accept the boundaries of behavior set for them by us and the law. Some teens will see a parent's rules or the law as a challenge. They may want to assert their own authority, to win their peers' acceptance, or to revel in the idea of "being bad" for its own sake. Simply put, this is rebellion. Paul argued that when God's laws were given, "sin" took advantage of the opportunity. The apostle explained that when someone is aware that it's wrong, for example, to covet, that sin produces all kinds of covetous desires in that person (Romans 7:8,11). When we tell a toddler, "Now don't touch Mommy's pretty new jewelry box," what does she do? Touch the thing! We should also pray that our teens accept the boundaries put on them by God, legal authorities, and us—that rebellion not even stir in our children.

A parent's biggest worry in this area is addiction—that our teens will become trapped by the addictive nature of these substances. Deuteronomy 12:30 says we should be careful not to be ensnared by inquiring about other gods. If we find our kids have experimented with an addictive substance, it's important to reiterate over and over the deadly physical effects alcohol, tobacco, and drugs can have on our bodies—and the damage or death we may inflict on others when we abuse. A good question to teach them to ask themselves is, Will I regret NOT using this today? The great risk of regret is if we do use these things, not if we don't. I pray, then, that my children remember those things we've taught them—that our instruction will ring in their ears louder than the whisper to rebel (Proverbs 22:6). I also pray that they remember the high purpose that God has for them and that they understand how substance abuse could affect their reaching that high purpose.

Prayer for Turning from Illegal Substances

Matthew 27:34; Exodus 23:2; Romans 7:8,11;
Deuteronomy 12:30; Romans 8:29

Lord, even you were tempted with a narcotic drink when you were on the cross. Thank you for your example of turning away from those things the Enemy would have us use to destroy our lives and our witness. Help me teach my child not to follow the crowd in doing wrong but instead choose to follow you. Help my teen to recognize the lies of the Enemy or the culture or the peer group that would lead toward illegal substances, such as drugs, alcohol, and tobacco. Strip away any root of rebellion that would produce sinful desires within him. May he not be trapped in a life of abuse and dependency but be solely dependent on your grace and mercy. Conform my child to the likeness of your son, Jesus Christ, so that he may become a model other kids will emulate. In Jesus' name, amen.

 ## Teens Talk

"I hold the views that I've been taught, but I also need to know what's with all the hype before I make a final decision."—Allison, age seventeen

"Smoking, drinking and drugs...my parents' mistake, not mine."—Jessica, age sixteen

God Talks

1. Read Romans 6:15-20.
2. What do you think it means to offer yourself to sin?
3. What is the eventual result of sin?
4. What are the results of obedience?
5. Read Romans 7:4-6. How can we make better choices in our lives when we're drawn to behavior that will hurt us?

 Others Talk

In *When Teens Stray: Parenting for the Long Haul,* Scott Larson suggests that parents lay out a process whereby they can make well-informed, nonemotionally charged, God-honoring decisions when they discover their kids' troubling behavior. He says that situations can be at one of three levels.

Dilemmas
- Ask how long the criminal activity or drug use has been going on (found cigarettes may not mean your daughter's addicted).
- Ponder, pray, ask for advice before making a decision.
- Ask yourself: *Can this be talked through?* Perhaps discussing the pros and cons of smoking will be enough to have her change her behavior.

Crises
These require more immediate and direct action.
- Ask yourself: What is the worst possible outcome of this behavior?
- Write down all the options and the pros and cons of each.
- Ask yourself: What is my responsibility? Keep the bulk of responsibility—as much as possible—on your child's shoulders. You

may need to arrange and pay for the drug rehab; the child eventually makes the decision to get well.

- Ask yourself: What is my objective? Our ultimate goals should be the spiritual and emotional growth of our children and the fulfillment of God's plan, not our escape from embarrassment.

Emergencies
These are 911, life-threatening events.
- Contact police or medical emergency personnel.
- Larson quotes R. A. Buddy Scott: "The battle over drugs or alcohol is rarely won without a residential treatment program.... Often a staged intervention by friends, family, and a therapist is necessary to get an adolescent into treatment. When confronted this way, 80 percent agree to get help."[51] Larson also lists help lines that can direct you to intervention services:

Focus on the Family, 1-800-A-FAMILY
The Minirth Clinic, 1-888-MINIRTH
Rapha, 1-800-383-4673
American Society of Addiction Medicine, 1-301-656-3920
Youth Crisis Hotline, 1-800-448-4663
National Drug Abuse Hotline, 1-800-662-4357[52]

You Talk

- Do you have questions about cigarettes, drugs, or alcohol that we could research together?
- What are some of the reasons teens you know smoke, take drugs, or drink?
- How do they feel about their addiction?
- How do you think I would feel (or do feel) about this?
- What do you think is God's perspective?

Chapter 21

Senioritis—Early Warning Stage for Arthritis

BURNOUT

The worst thing the University of California ever did for me was send me my acceptance letter early in January in my senior year of high school. Whoooooeeee! I was DONE! Just hand me my cap and gown and I was outta there! No more chemistry or Algebra II—I was headed on a road trip down Freedom Highway!

There was one problem. I still had five more months of school left, and I hadn't yet realized that I was *conditionally* accepted—that my senior grades still mattered to the University of California. A few states away on that Freedom Highway the road signs began to look a little bleary. All of a sudden Algebra II problems looked like hieroglyphics. I couldn't remember one lab from another as I tried to catch up on reports for chemistry. The only conversational phrase I could say in Russian was "I love you" (Craig and I had started to date). I put the brakes on that freedom vehicle and headed for homework.

A week before graduation I learned that I was in the top ten of my graduating class of 406. To determine the valedictorian and salutatorian, we ten students had to get our final grades. I knew I needed a serious strategy as I approached my teachers. I started with my P.E. teacher, Miss Johnson. She loved me. I had started the school's first girls' tennis team. My friend Janice and I had a perfect record: 2-0. Both of the other schools were no-shows. Easy A from Miss Johnson.

Then I headed for my English teachers. I had two English classes—science fiction and short stories. My former journalism teacher taught the sci-fi class. He loved me, and even though I had decided I hated science fiction, another easy A. Same from the short stories teacher.

Three down, four to go. These were tougher: Spanish, Russian, Algebra II, and chemistry. I headed for Spanish next, because I'd always gotten A's in Spanish. Besides, I'd taken enchiladas into class recently, and enchiladas should count for something. Yessssss! Another A.

Russian was tougher. This was just a semester course—a *taste* of borscht, so to speak. But Mr. Thornock was impressed when I told him "I love you" in Russian, and another A landed on my grade report.

The last two classes were going to be rough. I had almost no idea what I was doing on my Algebra II final, and my makeup lab reports were probably still in my chemistry teacher's basket.

When I approached my Algebra II teacher with the grade report, his eyes swept over the other grades. "Wow, five A's here. Good job, Miss Holm!" Without checking his grade book, he planted another A on my sheet.

Trying not to look too shocked, I thanked him and headed for the chem lab. Mr. Winter towered over me in his clean, crisp white lab coat and frowned when I asked for my grade.

"You missed class again yesterday, Miss Holm," he said as he looked at his grade book.

"Yes, I'm sorry. I had another senior class meeting. We're planning baccalaureate, you know." I looked at the ceiling, folded my hands, and started humming, "Kum-ba-yah, my Lord, kum-ba-yah..." I needed the

Lord's presence at that moment as I trembled before the toughest teacher in the high school.

"Well, this is too bad. Six perfect A's and I'm going to ruin your record."

Kum-ba-yah, my Lord, kum-ba-yah... I closed my eyes, waiting for the verdict. I'd been caught speeding by the highway patrol on my Freedom Ride, and I needed a huge gift of mercy as the officer wrote up my ticket.

Mr. Winters cleared his throat. "Well, you deserve a D," he said, "but I can't give you a D with all these A's here. You get a C. Good luck in college, Miss Holm. I hope you don't have to take chemistry."

Whew! Relief! I might not make valedictorian or runner-up, but a C in Chemistry would get me into the University of California.

As a high school teacher now, I try to recognize the early signs of seni'oritis and encourage the seniors to hang in there and get the job done so they can be proud of their record when they leave. "Do your best," I tell them. "Don't have regrets." I don't necessarily share my story with them (it might give them another rationalization), but I try to help them postpone their own Freedom Highway trips.

If your teen is a senior—or about to be—you might need to pray he or she won't get exhausted. Kids who are diligent students may also be holding down part-time jobs, doing sports or other activities, writing college and scholarship essays, finishing senior projects, and facing strenuous College Board Advanced Placement and other placement exams in English and math. Trust me: High school is a lot harder than when you and I were sitting in those chairs. They will be better ready for life when they graduate, that is, if they can make it that far. Pray that your teens and their friends can pace themselves through all these hoops and learn to cut back or seek help if that's feasible. When Moses was struggling in leadership, his father-in-law, Jethro, said, "What you are doing is not good. You and these people who come to you will only wear yourselves out. The work is too heavy for you; you cannot handle it alone" (Exodus 18:17-18). Of course, we parents can help guide our kids so they don't commit to too many activities, but we also can pray with and for them about the various things weighing on them.

Some teens may feel complacent, as I did. They may feel their college future is set, so why keep working at something they're going to leave behind anyway? In the parable of the rich fool, he says to himself, "You have plenty of good things laid up for many years. Take life easy; eat, drink and be merry" (Luke 12:19). But God has work for each and every day of our lives. He answered the man: "You fool! This very night your life will be demanded from you" (verse 20). We can ask God to help our teens realize that every moment of our lives matters to God—he will always want us to glorify him with whatever we're doing. Pray against mediocrity.

Some teens may not be burned out but instead feel frustrated, uncertain, or even fearful. Perhaps they didn't get into the college they most desired or aren't sure what to do. Like Job they may feel their "days have passed" with plans "shattered" (Job 17:11). They may be angry and decide to quit trying. Life ahead may look pretty uncertain if they only look at what the world seems to be offering. In such a circumstance we parents can pray that they'll wait for the "perfect gift…from above, coming down from the Father of the heavenly lights, who does not change like shifting shadows" (James 1:17). We can come alongside them by praying that they will learn to trust even in their uncertainty—"not knowing what will happen"—because they will want to "finish the race and complete the task the Lord Jesus has given" them (Acts 20:22,24).

Or maybe they're feeling a little scared—not ready to face the challenges of a four-year university or army boot camp or life on their own with full-time work and lots of living expenses. We've seen this lack of confidence in some of the people in the Bible. Moses prayed, "Who am I, that I should go to Pharaoh?" (Exodus 3:11). Jeremiah said, "I do not know how to speak; I am only a child" (Jeremiah 1:6). A cornerstone of prayer for this issue is that our children will know—as God told both Moses and Jeremiah—that they do not go alone but that God is with them (Exodus 3:12; Jeremiah 1:7-8). Our abilities do not matter as much as our faithful obedience to and trust in the God who has brought us to that place in life—and we parents can pray that our kids will know this truth as they approach their future outside our homes.

Prayer for Burnout
Exodus 18:17-18; Job 17:11; James 1:16-17; Acts 20:24;
Exodus 3:12; Jeremiah 1:7-8

Lord, I see symptoms of burnout in my child. She works long hours with many tasks still to finish. Help my teen balance and prioritize and delegate so she does not wear herself out. May she use her time well and not become complacent about her commitments. When life's circumstances—especially relating to important future plans—disappoint, I ask that my child not see shattered desires but your redirection instead. You do not change like shifting shadows but instead provide every good and perfect gift. Help my child adjust her thinking to accept your change of plans. I know that you can help her finish the race and finish those tasks you have called her to do. When my child feels inadequate, even fearful, I know you will be with her—and that you are enough. In Jesus' name, amen.

 Teens Talk

"Stress builds up in school."—Brett, age eighteen

"It's hard. I need breaks, or else my body tells me I need them."—Allison, age seventeen

God Talks

1. Read Exodus 18:13-27.
2. Why was Moses burned out?
3. Reread verses 17 and 18. Who else did Jethro say would become worn out? For what reason(s) could that be possible?
4. What might have been possible if Moses had continued on the same course?
5. Moses was told to delegate responsibility. What are some other ways to make our lives simpler?

 ## Others Talk

Senioritis or burnout is normal. Depression and suicide are not. According to the National Mental Health Association, suicide is the leading cause of death in adolescents and the second leading cause of death among college-age youth. Four out of five teens who attempt suicide have given clear warnings, which include:

- suicide threats, direct and indirect
- obsession with death
- poems, essays, and drawings that refer to death
- dramatic change in personality or appearance
- irrational, bizarre behavior
- overwhelming sense of guilt, shame, or reflection
- changed eating or sleeping patterns
- severe drop in school performance
- giving away belongings

If these signs are apparent in your teen, the NMHA suggests the following:

- Offer help and listen. Encourage depressed teens to talk about their feelings. Listen, don't lecture.

- Trust your instincts. If it seems the situation may be serious, promptly seek help. Break a confidence, if necessary, to save a life.
- Pay attention to talk about suicide. Ask direct questions, and don't be afraid of frank discussions. Silence is deadly!
- Seek professional help. It is essential to seek expert advice from a mental health professional who has experience in helping depressed teens. Also, alert key adults in the teen's life—family, friends, and teachers.[53]

 ## Others Talk

Self-mutilation is another alarming phenomenon appearing in about 1 percent of the American population, mostly teenage girls.[54] Also referred to as self-injury or self-abuse, it is a label for the practice of hurting oneself intentionally as a method of dealing with stress, depression, or overwhelming emotions or conditions (such as abuse). Self-mutilation manifests itself in cutting (making cuts in one's body with sharp objects), bruising, burning, and other forms of self-inflicted pain. Typically girls hurt themselves physically to distract themselves from their emotional pain.

Karen Conterio and Wendy Lader are directors of S.A.F.E. Alternatives (Self-Abuse Finally Ends) in the Chicago area—the first in-patient treatment center in the country for those who physically harm themselves. In their book *Bodily Harm* they list several warning signs, including scars on the arms or legs, repeated abrasions, secrecy, emotional distancing, frequent disappearances, weak excuses for the wounds, long sleeves or pants worn in warm weather, withdrawal, and difficulty handling regular responsibilities.[55]

Their suggestions for this phenomenon, which is usually not a precursor to suicide, include the following:

- Pay swift attention to the situation.
- Assure the adolescent that she won't be punished.

- Focus on getting the self-injurer to acknowledge her problem.
- Get her professional help (the authors can make referrals through their Web site at www.self-injury.com).
- If the adolescent refuses help, suggest that if the behavior is not really a problem, this will be confirmed by someone who isn't emotionally invested in proving anything (the professional counselor).
- Do whatever you can to make the injurer aware that she is not the only person affected by her behavior. Once the self-injurer understands the impact she's making on others, her resistance will erode, and she will be motivated to change.
- Adopt a collaborative plan with school officials.
- Talk to the injurer about what she wants others to know.[56]

You Talk

- What in your life is creating stress for you?
- How do you feel about that?
- In what ways do others or I contribute to any burnout you may be experiencing?
- Can you think of ways to simplify your life to make things less stressful?
- Is there something you or I could do that would help?

Chapter 22

Here Is the Church, There Is the Steeple...Where Is My Son?

FAITH

Look to the left.
Look to the right.
Stand up. Sit down.
Fight, fight, fight!

It wasn't a fall football game. It was another Sunday at church, my son was missing, and I was mad!

"I'll meet you there," he had said from his bed when I had left home for Sunday school with the two younger kids.

But worship was now well under way, and there was no sign of my tall, handsome, red-headed Justin. Church was not an option in our family, so I was praying, "Lord, wherever Justin is, make it clear to him that you are Lord and worthy of his worship." I was picturing the bedroom walls falling down around him or some such thing.

Concentrating on the sermon was difficult as I fled into prayer every few minutes to keep my concern in check. Imagine, then, my surprise when Justin walked up to me holding our youngest, Bethany.

"Don't tell me you've been here the whole time," I said.

Bethany answered for him. "No, Mommy, he was with me...in the nursery. We watched the Joshua movie and made the walls fall down."

Instead of his bedroom walls falling down, the LEGO walls in the nursery had. I glanced at my son with a sense of knowing. Spending time with his sister and her little buddies in nursery duty was more interesting than listening to another sermon. Maybe it was okay for my shy guy to encourage prebelievers in this way.

I remember the longest walk of his life. He was nine years old and had inched the forty feet from the back of our small church sanctuary to the pastor's feet at the end of the service to announce that he had put his life into Christ's hands. He was the youngest of his peers to do so—and the first of any boy in our church that I could remember in the nine years we'd been attending. He had made the decision all by himself.

His earlier faith decision was an eyeopener—literally. I'd taken the kids to the optometrist's for the first time. One kid was nearsighted. Another kid was farsighted. But instead of getting glasses, my kids were sent home with trial exercises. At first I pictured them doing up, down, up, down stretches and left, right, left, right swings, but their exercises were like this: Look at your homework, don't, look at your homework, don't. My kids liked this doctor. He told them that they were studying too long, reading too intensely. They were now supposed to stop looking at those pages in their books and homework sheets! What a prescription for a kid: Don't study!

That's exaggerating a tad, of course, but the day turned out to be life changing for Justin, because he said he felt God directing him on our return trip home to put his life in his hands. So he did. God opened his eyes and showed himself to be trustworthy. Justin asked God to come into his life, and God did. No big bangs or fireworks—but in the following years it seemed as though Justin's eyes were seeing life with sharper edges, rather than as a fuzzy Impressionistic painting. As the years went by, he realized that Christians often don't live their lives as transformed beings. However, these scenes weren't so pretty as the ones I'd seen with my new glasses. Instead, his new sight found ugly hypocrisy.

Christian husbands and wives didn't seem to get along any better than those who didn't profess Christ. They didn't behave any better in the workplace. They even turned against their own within the church walls, gossiping and alienating one another. Eventually my young man decided church didn't work. He knows God is real and that God works...but church is on hold for this stage of his life.

So, here is the church, here is the steeple...but where is my son? He's somewhere living on the edge of God's mercy—questioning his faith and that of others, finding the world has no answers and offers only transitory contentment—and he's finding his prodigal way back. He knows how to get home. He knows he'll be welcomed. However, I think he's still wondering if he can live with the church with his eyes wide open—if the leaves will be newly pretty or if they'll be a little gray and fuzzy. I pray they'll be beautiful.

Although Justin hasn't abandoned his faith, other teens do. Why? Tom Bisset offers four specific reasons and then one general one. We'll look at the specific reasons first:

- They have troubling, unanswered questions about their faith.
- Their faith isn't working for them.
- Other things in life become more important than their faith.
- They never personally owned their own faith.[57]

Each of these specific reasons can become a cornerstone in a structure of prayer.

We can pray that our kids find answers to those questions that hang them up in their faith and that we can be part of their faith-building process. You know what those questions are. Why does God allow suffering? Why aren't my prayers answered? How can Christ be the only way to salvation and eternal life? Paul told his trainee Timothy to study the

Scriptures (2 Timothy 3:14-17). The counsel from God's Word, as well as reliable books and teachers, can build a young person's faith. Thus my prayer is often that my own teaching will be strong and that my kids will seek out their answers in the Bible and other good sources.

Young people can often think that life's disappointments mean that Christianity doesn't work. Sometimes their prayers aren't answered the way they think they should be. Sometimes they're hurt by others or circumstances. We can pray that our kids will be able to endure hardship (2 Timothy 2:3) and be prepared for the struggles they'll certainly encounter over the years (2 Timothy 4:2). We'll also want to ask God to guard their hearts against false teachers (1 Timothy 1:3) and to equip them (2 Timothy 4:5) to weigh lies against the truth.

Many distractions can pull a teen away from the church. Sports tournaments may be scheduled on Sunday mornings. Late Saturday night gatherings can make kids too tired to get up the next day. Non-Christian friends can make fun of faith-related practices, such as prayer and Bible study. Intercede for your teen to receive positive reinforcement for his or her spiritual life. You can pray through 1 Timothy 4:12: "Don't let anyone look down on you because you are young, but set an example for the believers in speech, in life, in love, in faith and in purity." Pray that your child will "pursue righteousness, godliness, faith, love, endurance and gentleness" (1 Timothy 6:11) and bring others along in that faith search.

Do you have a peace about your child's personal commitment to Christ? Is your child's faith personal, or has your child been sliding along on your coattails? While Timothy's grandmother Lois and mother, Eunice, were believers, his father was not. Paul may have had doubts about Timothy's faith and leadership qualities (1 Corinthians 16:10-11), but eventually he was able to write, "I have no one else like him" (Philippians 2:20). As Timothy eventually had to prove his faith in the field, so will our kids; we can ask our Lord to display his unlimited patience for our children who will believe on him, receive eternal life, and work out their own faith throughout their lifetime (1 Timothy 1:16).

Bisset writes that the ultimate reason people leave the Christian faith is that they have "a failed or failing relationship with Jesus Christ"—at some point in time they stopped depending on Christ and started depending on something or someone else.[58] When David handed over the throne to his son Solomon, David told Solomon that the Lord God would not fail him or forsake him (1 Chronicles 28:20). Pray that your child passionately pursues his or her relationship with Christ, does not turn to other things that taint his or her worship, and understands that the Lord God does not fail or forsake those who love him.

Prayer for My Child's Faith
Mark 12:30; 1 Timothy 1:3; 2 Timothy 3:2-5; 1 Chronicles 28:20;
1 Timothy 4:8; 2 Timothy 2:3,2; 4:2

Father, I trust you for my child's faith and relationship with you. I acknowledge the desire to have my children reflect positively on my parenting abilities—especially in this area of faith. I give up and trust you for such expectations as church attendance, youth group commitment, and even personal, spiritual disciplines. More than anything I want my child to love you with all his heart, soul, mind, and strength. As his faith is growing, Lord, I ask you to guard him from negative, ungodly influences and instead to direct godly people to him who will encourage and teach him. Remind him that because you will not fail or forsake him, he can be strong and courageous in his faith. Guide my child, Father, as he seeks to be godly so that he can endure the hardships that are certain to fall in his path and so that he can teach, correct, and encourage others in their faith. In Jesus' name, amen.

Teens Talk

"Don't force religion on me. I will probably follow your steps if you don't force me."—Ephraim, age sixteen

"Just because I skip an hour of church for some reason doesn't mean that I don't believe."—Zak, age sixteen

 ## God Talks

1. Read 1 Timothy 4:7-16.
2. Make a list of the specific directions Paul gave to Timothy.
3. What do you think were the most important suggestions that could build Timothy's faith?
4. In 1 Timothy 4:12, Paul tells Timothy, "Don't let anyone look down on you because you are young." Why do you think adults tend to minimize the faith of teenagers?
5. Pray for specific ways that you could encourage your teen in his or her faith development.

 ## Others Talk

In *Why Christian Kids Leave the Faith,* Tom Bisset offers the good news that 85 percent of even the most severely rebellious dropouts return to their parents' faith and values by the time they are twenty-four years old[59] and that those figures probably increase as individuals age. He suggests that parents can help their children develop a faith that endures by doing the following:

- Since most spiritual breakdowns occur from the early teens to early twenties, during this time give your children your time and interest, show them your love, seek honesty and intimacy, talk with your kids, and teach and model as best you can what it means to be a Christian.

- During the college years—a possible "returning curve"—reach out to those who have rejected their faith, reopen the lines of communication, and find the family love and intimacy that dropouts often say was missing when they were younger. Be interested in their lives, talk, do things together—knowing that they may be rethinking their faith.
- Another door to spiritual renewal may occur as their own children are growing, especially if their kids become rebellious. Be aware that they may be looking again with renewed interest and openness at spiritual matters.[60]

You Talk

- How do you feel about your relationship with God?
- Have I pushed my faith on you? Do you feel your faith is your own?
- If you could change anything about our church or the Christian faith, what would those things be?
- What questions do you have about Christianity?
- How could I be a better example to you as a Christian?

If This Is So Great,
Why Am I Groaning?

There was absolutely nothing funny about my four labor experiences. I was fat. I was exhausted. Each of our babies was late, so each labor was induced with Pitocin. Sometimes that hurries up labor…but not in my case. I guess each kid wanted to make a dramatic entrance.

Bethany's was particularly memorable. I'd had a miserable morning, afternoon, and evening. The doctor had put in a full day and wanted to take his wife out for their anniversary. My nurse coach had put in her full shift and more.

"Before I go," she said, "I just want to check you one more time."

After the next contraction she measured me and announced, "Doctor! She's at nine!"

This was my history. Take a whole day to dilate a couple of centimeters, then whoosh right to delivery.

When the nurse spoke, I distinctly remember thinking, *I'm at nine centimeters. I can push now.* So I did.

Trying to pull on rubber gloves, which don't slip on easily over just-washed hands, the doctor looked over at me and said, "No, Janet, don't push yet!"

Right. As all of you mothers know, you don't just stop pushing once you've started. Besides, by that time, Bethany Anne McHenry had decided she'd finally show up.

I think I probably announced the fact to the entire West Coast with my "I HAVE TO!"

Coach Connie stepped in for the intended receiver and caught the ball…I mean baby, who arrived with one push. Other than the fact that I had a retained placenta and almost needed emergency surgery to save my life, things went peachy, and we've laughed since then about the traumas of the day.

Just as we learn to laugh about labor and laugh about the silly things our toddlers say, someday we begin to laugh again after our kids have grown through their teen trials. We look at old photos and giggle about hairdos and clothing styles and the antics they put us through. Laughing doesn't minimize the pain or slight the memories. It shows that God is in control and that by entrusting our kids and their issues to him, we've done the best thing we could do. It's joy, really—celebrating the passing of our teens from adolescence to adulthood.

Through my funny stories I hope I've come alongside you and encouraged you. With the scriptures and prayers I hope I gave you ammunition for your own struggles with your teen. With the other helps I hope I've provided practical ways to meet those very real needs you're experiencing in your home. Ultimately, I hope you will see that prayer should be a first response, not a last resort, as you're raising your teenager. It's not the *only*, last-ditch thing we can do; prayer is the best thing we can do. Because we're entrusting the Sovereign One to take care of our teenager. Because he not only has the answer—he is the Answer. And because, after hours and hours on your knees, you will find that God has honored those prayers and changed your child. Not only is he trustworthy to take care of our needs with our children, he is the giver of hope and joy. We will not only survive through our prayers but also thrive with the peace he will instill in us for trusting him.

I have one last resource for you—Kevin Leman's "A Teenager's Ten Commandments to Parents" from his book *Adolescence Isn't Terminal:*

1. Please don't give me everything I say I want. Saying no shows me you care. I appreciate guidelines.
2. Don't treat me as if I were a little kid. Even though you know what's "right," I need to discover some things for myself.
3. Respect my need for privacy. Often I need to be alone to sort things out and daydream.
4. Never say, "In my day…" That's an immediate turnoff. Besides, the pressures and responsibilities of my world are more complicated than they were when you were my age.
5. I don't pick your friends or clothes; please don't criticize mine. We can disagree and still respect each other's choices.
6. Refrain from always rescuing me; I learn most from my mistakes. Hold me accountable for the decisions I make in life; it's the only way I'll learn to be responsible.
7. Be brave enough to share your disappointments, thoughts, and feelings with me. By the way, I'm never too old to be told I'm loved.
8. Don't talk in volumes. I've had years of good instruction; now trust me with the wisdom you have shared.
9. I respect you when you ask me for forgiveness for a thoughtless deed or word on your part. It proves that neither of us is perfect.
10. Set a good example for me as God intended you to do. I pay more attention to your actions than your words.[61]

I'd just add one more, in the form of a prayer that perhaps your teen could say someday:

> Lord, please let Mom and Dad know that the best thing they can
> do is pray for me. My life is tough. My friends all want to look
> perfect. I'm expected to get perfect grades. The teachers and
> coaches demand perfect behavior. Most days I feel dumb and ugly

and would just like to sleep all day long to avoid the prospect of messing up. I know it's important to talk with your parents about how you feel, but sometimes I just don't feel like doing that. So, I'm thinking, Lord, could you just remind my folks to pray for me today? For my classes and tests. For my friends—that we'll all just get along. For me, so I have the strength to live out my faith the way I know you want me to. Thanks for listening, God.

Pray for your teenagers, entrusting them to his care. Then know that he will meet each and every need in his perfect way.

Recommended Reading for Parents of Teens

Arp, David, and Claudia Arp. *Suddenly They're 13 or the Art of Hugging a Cactus: A Parent's Survival Guide for the Adolescent Years.* Grand Rapids: Zondervan, 1999.

Beausay, Bill. *Teenage Boys! Shaping the Man Inside: Surviving and Enjoying These Extraordinary Years.* Colorado Springs: WaterBrook, 1998.

Bernstein, Neil I. *How to Keep Your Teenager Out of Trouble and What to Do If You Can't.* New York: Workman Publishing, 2001.

Berry, Richard L. *Angry Kids: Understanding and Managing the Emotions That Control Them.* Grand Rapids: Revell, 2001.

Bisset, Tom. *Why Christian Kids Leave the Faith.* Grand Rapids: Discovery House, 1992.

Carlson, Melody, Heather Kopp, and Linda Clare. *Lost Boys and the Moms Who Love Them: Encouragement and Hope for Dealing with Your Wayward Son.* Colorado Springs: WaterBrook, 2002.

Chapman, Gary. *The Five Love Languages of Teenagers.* Chicago: Northfield, 2000.

Cloud, Henry, and John Townsend. *Boundaries with Kids: When to Say YES, When to Say NO, to Help Your Children Gain Control of Their Lives.* Grand Rapids: Zondervan, 1998.

Dobson, James. *Bringing Up Boys: Practical Advice and Encouragement for Those Shaping the Next Generation of Men.* Wheaton, Ill.: Tyndale, 2001.

Dockrey, Karen. *When a Hug Won't Fix the Hurt: Walking Your Child Through Crisis.* Birmingham, Ala.: New Hope Publishers, 2000.

Dudman, Martha Tod. *Augusta, Gone: A True Story.* New York: Simon and Schuster, 2001.

Eldridge, Sherrie. *Twenty Things Adopted Kids Wish Their Adoptive Parents Knew.* New York: Dell, 1999.

Graham, Ruth Bell. *Prodigals [and Those Who Love Them].* Grand Rapids: Baker, 2001.

Hersh, Sharon A. *"Mom, I Feel Fat!" Becoming Your Daughter's Ally in Developing a Healthy Body Image.* Colorado Springs: Shaw, 2001.

Heyman, Richard. *How to Say It to Teens: Talking About the Most Important Topics of Their Lives.* Paramus, N.J.: Prentice Hall, 2001.

Larson, Scott. *When Teens Stray: Parenting for the Long Haul.* Ann Arbor: Servant, 2002.

Laurent, Robert. *Bringing Your Teen Back to God.* Elgin, Ill.: David C. Cook, 1991. Out of print.

Leman, Kevin. *Adolescence Isn't Terminal.* Wheaton, Ill.: Tyndale, 2002.

McMahon, Tom. *Teen Tips: A Practical Survival Guide for Parents with Kids 11 to 19.* New York: Pocket Books, 1996.

Morrison, Jan. *A Safe Place: Hope and Healing for Teens, A Guide for Living Beyond Abuse.* Colorado Springs: Shaw, 2002.

Narramore, Bruce. *Adolescence Is Not an Illness: A Book for Parents.* Old Tappan, N.J.: Revell, 1980. Out of print.

Nelsen, Jane, and Lynn Lott. *Positive Discipline for Teenagers: Empowering Your Teens and Yourself Through Kind and Firm Parenting.* Roseville, Calif.: Prima Publishing, 2000.

Omartian, Stormie. *The Power of a Praying Parent.* Eugene, Ore.: Harvest House, 1995.

Peretti, Frank. *The Wounded Spirit.* Nashville: Word, 2000.

Pipher, Mary. *Reviving Ophelia: Saving the Selves of Adolescent Girls.* New York: Ballantine, 2002.

Ruppert, Martha. *The Dating Trap: Helping Your Children Make Wise Choices in Their Relationships.* Chicago: Moody Press, 2000.

Smalley, Gary, and Greg Smalley. *Bound by Honor: Fostering a Great Relationship with Your Teen.* Wheaton, Ill.: Tyndale, 1998.

Smith, Annette. *Help! My Little Boy's Growing Up: Guiding Your Son Through the Maze of Adolescence.* Eugene, Ore.: Harvest House, 2002.

————, *Help! My Little Girl's Growing Up: Guiding Your Daughter Through Her Physical and Emotional Changes.* Eugene, Ore.: Harvest House, 2001.

Weidmann, Jim, Janet Weidmann, J. Otis Ledbetter; and Gail Ledbetter. *Spiritual Milestones: A Guide to Celebrating Your Children's Spiritual Passages.* Colorado Springs: Cook Communications, 2001.

White, Joe, and Jim Weidmann, eds. *Parents' Guide to the Spiritual Mentoring of Teens: Building Your Child's Faith Through the Adolescent Years.* Wheaton, Ill.: Tyndale, 2001.

Wright, H. Norman. *Pre-Hysteric Parenting: The Frazzled Parent's Guide to Harmony in the Home, Replacing Indulgence with Responsibility.* Colorado Springs: Cook Communications, 2001.

Yates, Susan Alexander. *And Then I Had Teenagers: Encouragement for Parents of Teens and Preteens.* Grand Rapids: Baker, 2001.

Recommended Reading for Teens

Bolton, Martha. *Saying Goodbye When You Don't Want To: Teens Dealing with Loss.* Ann Arbor: Servant, 2002.

Clark, Jeramy. *I Gave Dating a Chance: A Biblical Perspective to Balance the Extremes.* Colorado Springs: WaterBrook, 2000.

Clark, Jeramy, and Jerusha Clark. *He's Hot, She's Hot: What to Look for in the Opposite Sex.* Colorado Springs: WaterBrook, 2001.

Fuller, Cheri, and Ron Luce. *When Teens Pray: Powerful Stories of How God Works.* Sisters, Ore.: Multnomah, 2002.

Gresh, Bob, and Dannah Gresh. *Who Moved the Goalpost? 7 Winning Strategies in the Sexual Integrity Game Plan.* Chicago: Moody, 2001.

Gresh, Dannah. *And the Bride Wore White: Seven Secrets to Sexual Purity.* Chicago: Moody, 1999.

Harris, Joshua. *I Kissed Dating Goodbye: A New Attitude Toward Romance and Relationships.* Sisters, Ore.: Multnomah, 1997.

Notes and Acknowledgments

1. From *Positive Discipline for Teenagers* by Jane Nelsen and Lynn Lott, copyright © 1994, 2000 by Jane Nelsen and Lynn Lott. Used by permission of Prima Publishing, a division of Random House, Inc.

2. Adapted from *Bound by Honor* by Gary Smalley and Greg Smalley, a Focus on the Family book published by Tyndale House Publishers. Copyright © 1998, Gary Smalley and Greg Smalley. All rights reserved. International copyright secured. Used by permission.

3. Found at www.missclick.chickclick.com/articles/301092p1.html. "What Do You Mean?" Missclick: A Snowball Network, 29 January 2002. This Web site has since been discontinued.

4. Found at www.chicagoparent.com/CP_pages/archive/ Interview%20Archive/Int0500.htm. Sharon Bloyd-Peshkin, "Swearing Off Foul Language," *Chicago Parent*, 9 February 2003.

5. Susan Alexander Yates, *And Then I Had Teenagers: Encouragement for Parents of Teens and Preteens* (Grand Rapids: Baker Book House Company, 2001), 116-27.

6. *Webster's Seventh New Collegiate Dictionary*, s.v. "idiot."

7. Shari M. Larson, e-mail interview, 25 September 2002. For more information about Moms In Touch, International, you can make contact through the following: P.O. Box 1120, Poway, CA 92074-1120; 1-800-949-6667 or 1-858-486-4065; or www.MomsInTouch.org.

8. California Department of Education, *Parents Are Teachers, Too* (Sacramento: California Department of Education, 1990).

9. Taken from *Suddenly They're 13*. Copyright © 1999 by David and Claudia Arp. Used by permission of Zondervan.

10. Found at www.nashvilleparent.com/features/0499/choreWars.html. Tricia Goyer, "Chore Wars," *Nashville Parent Magazine,* 12 March 2000.

11. Found at www.parentingteens.about.com/library/weekly/aa070500a.htm. Denise Witmer, "Teenagers and Sleep," Parenting of Adolescents, 5 March 2002.

12. Found at www.smmc.com/sleep/teen.html. Richard Simon Jr., M.D., "Teens and Sleep," Sleep Disorders Center, 5 March 2002.

13. Found at www.ojp.usdoj.gov/bjs/cvict_c.htm. "Crime Characteristics," U.S. Department of Justice, Bureau of Justice Statistics, 20 December 2001.

14. Found at www.ojp.usdoj.gov/bjs/cvict_v.htm. "Victim Characteristics," U.S. Department of Justice, Bureau of Justice Statistics, 19 February 2001.

15. Excerpted from *How to Keep Your Teenager Out of Trouble.* Copyright © 2001 Neil Bernstein. Used by permission of Workman Publishing Co., Inc., New York. All rights reserved.

16. Tom McMahon, *Teen Tips: A Practical Survival Guide for Parents with Kids 11 to 19* (New York: Pocket, 1996), 101.

17. Nelsen and Lott, *Positive Discipline for Teenagers,* 251.

18. Janet Bodnar, "Helping Teens Stretch Earnings," *Sacramento Bee,* 23 July 2000, D4.

19. Brad Lewis, "Trendsetting Preteens," *Focus on the Family Magazine* (August 2001): 15.

20. Found at www.faithworks.com/articles/article%20archive/pierce.htm. Greg Warner, "Stigma: Pierced Christians Say Many Misjudge the Motive for Their Markings," 23 March 2003.

21. Bernstein, *Keep Your Teenager Out of Trouble,* 365-8.

22. Adapted from *Lyrics Don't Matter* by Jerry Melchisedeck, published by Focus on the Family. Copyright © 1999 Focus on the Family. All rights reserved. International copyright secured. Used by permission.

23. Found at www.drkutner.com/articles/telephone.html. Lawrence Kutner, "Insights for Parents: Teenagers and Telephones," Lawrence Kutner, Ph.D., 20 June 2002.

24. Kutner, "Insights for Parents."

25. Found at www.ldolphin.org/lust.html. Anonymous, "The War Within Continues," Christianity Today International, 21 March 2001.

26. Found at www.afa.net/pornography/sg121500.asp. Steve Gallagher, "Devastated by Internet Porn," American Family Online, 15 December 2000.

27. Michael Craven, Center for Decency, e-mail correspondence, 21 October 2002.

28. Elizabeth Kemper and Mark Ivey, "Get Serious About Online Controls" and "Setting Limits for Kids on Computers," Sacramento Bee, 26 August 2001 and 24 February 2002.

29. Found at www.sikids.com/sportsparents/psychology/frazzled.html. Pamela Hill Nettleton, "Frazzled Parents: Do Your Kids' Sports Rule Your Life?" Sports Parents, 28 June 2002. Also, www.sikids.com/sportsparents/ psychology/frazzled.html. Mickey Rathbun, "How to Help Your Child Juggle Sports, School, and Life," Sports Parents, 28 June 2002.

30. Dorothy Korber, "Warning Sounded on Prom Parties," Sacramento Bee, 2 May 2000, A1,9.

31. Sharon Hersh, "Mom, I Feel Fat!" (Colorado Springs: Shaw, 2001), 157-8.

32. Found at www.nationaleatingdisorders.org/p.asp?WebPage_ ID=286& Profile_ID=41141. "Bulimia Nervosa," National Eating Disorders Association, 27 July 2002, 2.

33. Found at www.nationaleatingdisorders.org/p.asp?WebPage_ ID=286& Profile_ID=41140. "Binge Eating Disorder," National Eating Disorders Association, 27 July 2002, 1.

34. Found at www.nationaleatingdisorders. "Binge Eating Disorder," "Bulimia Nervosa," "Anorexia Nervosa."

35. Margo Maine, Father Hunger: Fathers, Daughters and Food (Carlsbad, Calif.: Gurze Books, 1991), 3, quoted in Hersh, "Mom, I Feel Fat!" 52.

36. Found at www.nationaleatingdisorders.org/p.asp?WebPage_ID=285. "Information for Boys and Men," National Eating Disorders Association, 23 October 2002.

37. Reprinted from *"Mom, I Feel Fat!"* Copyright © 2001 by Sharon A. Hersh. WaterBrook Press, Colorado Springs, CO. All rights reserved.

38. Real words from the *Balderdash* game, Gameworks Creations, Inc., 1984.

39. Richard L. Berry, *Angry Kids: Understanding and Managing the Emotions That Control Them* (Grand Rapids: Revell, a division of Baker Book House Company, 2001), 52-61.

40. Adapted from Joshua Harris, *I Kissed Dating Goodbye: A New Attitude Toward Romance and Relationships* (Sisters, Ore.: Multnomah, 1997), 205-20.

41. Harris, *I Kissed Dating Goodbye,* 219.

42. Jeramy Clark, *I Gave Dating a Chance: A Biblical Perspective to Balance the Extremes* (Colorado Springs: WaterBrook, 2000), 90-7.

43. Kevin Leman, *Adolescence Isn't Terminal* (Wheaton, Ill.: Tyndale, 2002), 159-61.

44. Yates, *And Then I Had Teenagers,* 170-82.

45. Barry Yeoman, "The Teen Report: Teenland," *Working Mother* (April 2001): 36.

46. Yeoman, " Teenland."

47. Yeoman, " Teenland."

48. Yeoman, " Teenland."

49. Yeoman, " Teenland."

50. "Teen Smoking Lowest in a Decade, Survey Shows," *Sacramento Bee,* 17 May 2002, A7.

51. R. A. Buddy Scott, *Relief for Hurting Parents: What to Do and How to Think When You're Having Trouble with Your Kids* (Nashville: Oliver Nelson, 1989), 220, quoted in Scott Larson, *When Teens Stray: Parenting for the Long Haul* (Ann Arbor, Mich.: Servant, 2002), 138.

52. Adapted from *When Teens Stray: Parenting for the Long Haul* by Dr. Scott Larson, © 2002 by Dr. Scott Larson. Published by Servant Publications, P.O. Box 8617, Ann Arbor, Michigan 48107. (www.servantpubl.com) Used with permission.

53. Found at www.nmha.org/infoctr/factsheets/82.cfm. National Mental Health Association, "Factsheet: Suicide—Teen Suicide," 14 August 2002, 1.

54. Found at www.teenagerstoday.com/resources/articles/mutilate.htm. Carma Haley Shoemaker, "A Cut Above: The Practice of Mutilation," iParenting Media, 18 March 2003.

55. Karen Conterio, Wendy Lader, and Jennifer Kingson Bloom, *Bodily Harm: The Breakthrough Healing Program for Self-Injurers* (New York: Hyperion, 1998), 161.

56. Conterio, Lader, and Bloom, *Bodily Harm,* 162-7.

57. This material is taken from *Why Christian Kids Leave the Faith,* by Tom Bisset. Copyright © 1992. Used by permission of Discovery House Publishers, Box 3566, Grand Rapids, Michigan 49501. All rights reserved.

58. Bisset, *Why Christian Kids Leave,* 214.

59. Bisset, *Why Christian Kids Leave,* 147.

60. Bisset, *Why Christian Kids Leave,* 149-51, 217.

61. From *Adolescence Isn't Terminal* by Kevin Leman © 2002. Used by permission of Tyndale House Publishers, Inc. All rights reserved.

About the Author

Janet Holm McHenry is the author of seventeen books, including the popular *PrayerWalk* and its companion book, *Daily PrayerWalk*. A founder of two prayer ministries, she has also spoken on radio shows and before audiences across the country. Other than prayerwalking, Janet says her favorite thing to do is to spend an evening with her husband, Craig, and their four great kids.

To contact Janet McHenry about her speaking or writing,
see her Web site:
www.dailyprayerwalking.com

Or write her at:
P.O. Box 750
Loyalton, CA 96118

To learn more about WaterBrook Press and view
our catalog of products, log on to our Web site:
www.waterbrookpress.com

WATERBROOK
PRESS

Challenge your body.
Feed your spirit.
Change the world.

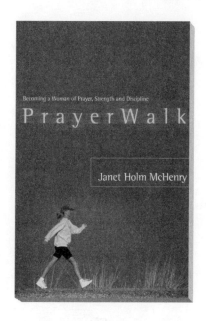

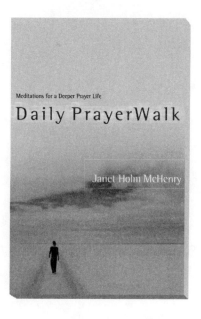

Learn how you can set out on a journey to increased energy, better health, and greater joy—and experience a rich, full prayer ministry that will have a lasting impact on your loved ones and community.

Raise the level of your walking and praying routine, whether you are a new or experienced prayerwalker or one who simply wants to challenge and strengthen your prayer practice.

Become physically *and* spiritually stronger with *PrayerWalk* and *Daily PrayerWalk* by Janet Holm McHenry.

 WATERBROOK PRESS